THE ART OF LIVING

Living within the Laws of Life

BENJAMIN CREME

Share International Foundation
Amsterdam • London • Los Angeles

*The cover picture is reproduced from a painting by
Benjamin Creme entitled **Soul-infusion** (1966).*

Dedication

This book is dedicated to
my revered Master.
His overshadowing presence
is its inspiration.

CONTENTS

PREFACE

In common with the two previous books, *The Great Approach* and *The Art of Co-operation*, *The Art of Living* is conceived as three separate but interconnected parts. Each part concludes with a range of questions and answers arising from the theme of the talk.

In Part One, 'The Art of Living', a commentary on an article by my Master and published in *Share International* magazine, Volume 25, No 1, 2006, the idea is presented that living is an art, as is painting or music. Like painting and music or any other art, therefore, living requires the understanding of and adherence to the laws and rules under which the art can flourish. This essentially new concept of living relates it to the great Law of Cause and Effect (the Law of Karma in the East) and the connected Law of Rebirth, the basic laws of our planetary existence. The correct understanding and following of these two laws are prerequisites for the creation of harmlessness in every sphere of our lives and thus also for the creation of right human relations, itself the prerequisite for human happiness. It is by the outer expression of the indwelling human soul through the intuition that this is finally achieved. We are entering an era in which great new energies will become available to us for such a flowering of the arts of all kinds, above all the art of living.

Part Two, 'The Pairs of Opposites', is a commentary on an article given by my Master and published in *Share International* magazine, Volume 22, No.1, 2003.

Historically, the evolution of humanity would seem to be one of almost constant warfare, aggression and hatred. With the discovery of the atomic bomb we have perfected our ability to destroy each other in large numbers and at great distances. Is this destructiveness, then, the true, essential nature of man? And if not, why has he behaved so consistently as if it were?

The answer lies in man's unique position in the evolution of the kingdoms on Earth, the meeting point of spirit and matter. Man, in essence, is an immortal soul, divinely perfect, immersed in matter. For long ages in the incarnational process, the inertia of the matter aspect precludes any significant expression of the soul's perfection. Eventually, the innate aspiration of man draws him upwards and onwards until the two poles of his nature gradually come together and are resolved in total union.

Then the perfected man realizes that the dichotomy between spirit and matter – their apparent opposition – is only seeming, in fact, illusion. He sees that they are different aspects of one perfect, divine Whole.

The long struggle to reach this revelation generates the friction and fire necessary for the journey, his aspiration lights for him the way. Thus does man fulfil his destined role on planet Earth: the spiritualization of matter.

Unlike Parts One and Two, which are commentaries on articles given by my Master for the magazine *Share International*, Part Three is inspired by some lines on illusion, given through Alice A. Bailey by the Master Djwhal Khul (DK), and quoted by Aart Jurriaanse in his compilation, *Ponder on This* (Lucis Press, 1971).

The talk reveals the unexpected fact that illusion is a soul activity, where the soul itself is blinded by the misinterpretations of ideas presented to it by the mental bodies of humanity. As glamour is illusion on the astral-emotional level, illusion *per se* is a condition of those who are more intellectually oriented. They flood the mental body with ideas and multitudes of thoughtforms that prevent the soul from experiencing reality.

Part Three covers the illusions of individuals, nations, governments and groups of all kinds. Wherever and whenever people misinterpret reality, through ignorance and spiritual short-sightedness, they create a block to the soul's vision, and live in illusion. The use of the intuition, a faculty of the soul, is seen as the only instrument that can clear the mental body of illusion. This requires a deepening of soul contact which is developed by correct meditation, mind control and a more intelligent understanding and practice of the laws of life. These are now being engaged in by growing numbers of people, and will lead eventually, under the stimulus of the Masters, to the freeing of humanity from the fogs of illusion.

Background Information

These lectures and answers to questions were addressed primarily to groups familiar with my information and previous publications. Therefore I speak freely about the Lord Maitreya and the Masters of Wisdom, without the need to explain Who They are, Their work and relation to humanity. For new readers, however, some explanation is essential and I offer the following brief account of Their work and plans.

The Masters of Wisdom are a group of perfected men Who have preceded us in evolution and indeed have reached a point where They need no further incarnation on our planet. Nevertheless, They remain on Earth to oversee the evolution of the rest of us. They are the Custodians of the evolutionary process, the Guides, the Mentors, the Protectors of the race, and work to fulfil the Plan of evolution of our Planetary Logos through humanity and the lower kingdoms. For many thousands of years They (and Their predecessors) have lived mainly in the remote mountain and desert areas of the world – the Himalaya, Andes, Rockies, Cascades, Carpathians, Atlas, Urals, and the Gobi and other deserts. From these mountain and desert retreats They have overseen and stimulated human evolution from behind the scenes.

For over 500 years They have prepared Themselves for a group return to the everyday world which, I submit, is now in progress. In July 1977, Their head and leader, the Lord Maitreya, Who embodies the Christ Principle (the energy of Love) and holds the office of World Teacher, descended from His Himalayan retreat and entered London, England, His 'point of focus' in the modern world. Maitreya lives in the Asian community of London as an 'ordinary' man awaiting the appropriate time to come openly before the world. He is expected by religious groups under different names: the Christ; the Imam Mahdi; the Messiah; Krishna; Maitreya Buddha. He does not come as a religious leader but as an educator in the broadest sense.

Maitreya's presence will galvanize humanity into making the necessary changes in our political, economic and social life which will guarantee peace, justice and freedom for all humanity. His major concern is the disparity in living standards between the developed and developing worlds, which, He says, threatens the future of the race. Recent terrorist activity is a symptom of these divisions. Maitreya sees the principle of sharing as the key to the solution of our manifold problems, and the means of bringing humanity into right relationship. Maitreya has said: "Take your brother's need as the measure for your action and solve the problems of the world. There is no other course." Soon Maitreya will be seen on major television in America (unannounced as Maitreya) and His open Mission will begin.

In January 1959 I was contacted by one of the Masters in the Himalaya and soon after by Maitreya, Himself. I was offered the task of preparing the way for Their emergence, creating the climate of hope and expectancy, a task on which I have been engaged now for 32 years. In the course of the training by my Master to prepare me for this work, we have established a moment-to-moment two-way telepathic link. This enables Him to communicate with me, with the minimum of His attention and energy. He forged an instrument through whom He could work, and which would be responsive to His slightest impression (of course, with my complete co-operation and without the slightest infringement of my free will). The Master's articles contained in this book were dictated by Him originally for *Share International* magazine.

Further information about Maitreya and the Masters can be found in my books and in *Share International* magazine and website, details of which are given at the end of this book.

I would like to express my gratitude to the many people in London, San Francisco and Los Angeles whose time and effort have contributed to this book. Their devotion to the tasks of editing, proofreading and indexing, cheerfully and efficiently undertaken, have made its publication possible. In particular, I would like to express my gratitude, once again, to Michiko Ishikawa for her invaluable work in organizing the copious material into readable form.

Benjamin Creme
London, March 2006

PART ONE

THE ART OF LIVING

*This chapter is based on an edited version of the keynote talk given by Benjamin Creme at the Transmission Meditation Conference held near San Francisco, USA, in August 2005. (First published in **Share International** magazine, January/February 2006.)*

This talk is about the art of living. It is probably the most important subject one could be talking about, although the vast majority of people on Earth have no idea that living is an art. Since it is an art, it does not just happen by chance. The laws and rules underlying the art must be understood and followed. Only then will we have a world in which all its inhabitants are living in right relationship, expressing their divinity, their potential Godhood. If we do not know that there are laws and rules, we end up as we are today and at all times previously, in a mess, a catastrophic situation, totally out of kilter with the idea of an art.

An art, whether painting, music or some other art, has to obey certain laws and rules. If you want to be a painter or composer, you have to learn the laws by which the art is formed; the methods too, but more profoundly the laws governing the qualities of art, like proportion, like revelation. The magic of art is stored in the obedience to these laws. Together with these laws are rules, which, in some cases, in some periods in history, have been followed literally for thousands of years without any apparent change. Some such pieces of art are produced now in religious groups under the same age-old canons – of beauty, righteousness and truth, canons of holiness and right relationship of man to God, and therefore of man to man.

For the most part, modern painters and composers have stretched the border of these canons and loosened them, and created art which, if it does obey the laws and rules of its medium, does so in a very cavalier fashion, haphazard and improvised, instinctive and not too well-developed. The art produced under this lack of canons is relatively superficial. That does not mean that it is bad art, but it is relatively superficial, not touching the depths of meaning pertaining to the highest form of art.

We are in a period of extreme disarray in our world – politically, economically and socially. We are all aware of it. Increasingly, the masses of people are becoming aware of it and are beginning to fret and feel the chaffing of these wrong structures, wrong laws, wrong habits – in other words, conditioning – and are seeking ways out of them. That is producing the upheaval which we see in the world today.

If you are a painter, you know that there are certain laws of proportion which, roughly speaking, most artists follow – if only instinctively – out of the habit of seeing them before in art that did follow the rules of composition, the laws of proportion. Even if it is a very conventional art, a very unoriginal product which is produced, if it obeys these laws to some extent, even instinctively, without much understanding, then that painting or piece of music is useful and interesting to someone. It may contain a tune that always pleases or have pretty colours and proportions that please the eye.

There can be no work of art produced at all under any circumstances that does not somehow obey a law, rule or procedure, however unknown. The better the artist, the more conscious he will be of that procedure and the better he will be at achieving his goals. The conventional artist will be satisfied at an early stage. The conventional art of any period, whether painting or music, is popular and does not tax the understanding of most people.

The painter starts with a canvas or board. He sets about covering it with coloured shapes or touches until it obeys the law of beauty according to his sense of what is beautiful, until it looks right, until everything is in its place, however conventional the image might be. Every angle and curve is related in the general rhythm of the picture. It has some kind of life, however conventional. A vibration comes from it which makes people buy it and put it on the wall. If it did not have that vibration, no one would buy the painting, however straightforward and conventional it was.

If you are a composer, you have to know what makes music work. You have to understand the laws of harmony and many other laws and properties of music, depending on the complexity of the work. You have to be able to score it. You have to look always for completion, for recognizing how far to go, how long or short the piece must be. Composers have experimented down the ages with lengths of composition, but whatever the length, they have to obey the laws of composition. They have to obey the laws of counterpoint, harmony, instrumentation and colour of sound. A tremendous, rich amount of knowledge goes into the production of a sophisticated piece of music, however conventional in terms of meaning it might be.

Yet, in life, people have no real education. If you want to be a painter, you either go to a school of art or to the studio of someone who is already mature in his development, and learn from him. Likewise, with musicians, they learn from each other. They go to a school of music and learn the rudiments. The rudiments are fundamentally the laws governing the production of a piece.

In education, we are taught to read and write, which, of course, is very important. We are taught a little bit of history, geography, arithmetic, mathematics generally, and that is about all. We are taught, to some extent, how to learn at least the concrete knowledge of our particular science or needed skill and that is all. We are not taught how to live, the art of living. There is no school where we can go to learn the art of living.

It is a spiritual problem because the art of living is tied up with living itself. It depends what you believe about the nature of life, how important you find it to go more deeply into the nature of living, or attempt to analyse and understand the essentials of life at any period of time.

We are living at an extraordinary time, a transitional period between two great ages, so that what seemed constant before is no longer constant. Knowledge that seemed certain is no longer certain. All we see is the past and possibly hints of the future, and we are torn, standing in the middle.

I would like to further this thought by reading an article that my Master wrote for *Share International* magazine.

Moving into Divinity

by the Master –, through Benjamin Creme

Throughout the world, men are beginning to realize that their long-held beliefs and certainties are less certain than they had supposed. The breakdown of their social and political institutions calls in question the value of their established ways of thinking, and presents men with a dilemma: the current modes of thought and action no longer seem to work; the future modes are, as yet, unclear. Thus it is that men stand undecided, awaiting guidance, lost in a vain attempt to maintain the past or to predict the future. In such situations, men are ripe for change.

Few there are who know the direction or the extent of the needed changes, nor how they may be accomplished, but, gradually, it is dawning on many that the present ways of living are bankrupt of meaning and lack all potential for human happiness. Large numbers thus 'opt out' of the struggle and seek solace and equilibrium in the growing number of religions, philosophies and 'cults', ancient and new. The changes needed seem too vast, too radical, for human hands or minds to set in motion, and they turn inwards to the God Who, they suspect, controls the affairs of men.

Did they but know it, they, themselves, are that very God, awaiting an opportunity to manifest. They, themselves, control their lives, for good or ill. It is they, by their actions, who turn the wheel of events, who engender conflict or peace, who sow mischief or goodwill.

Men must learn their role and innate power in life and take, thus, responsibility for its quality and direction. Unless they do this they will never leave their infancy behind.

Maitreya enters now the world arena to teach men that they are Gods in potential, that they are powerful, indeed, and that conditioning, alone, holds them in thrall to superstition and fear, competition and greed. He will show men the way to renounce the past, and to construct, under His wise guidance, a civilization worthy of men who are moving into their Divinity. The day is not far off when men will hear His Call, and hearing, respond. The day is not far off when men will know that the long dark night is over, that the time has come to welcome the new light which has entered the world.

Thus will men begin the task of reconstruction, a task which demands the strength and will of all. All must see this time as an opportunity to serve and grow, to fulfil the destiny which has brought them into the world now.

When, in future times, men look back to these climactic days, they will wonder with astonishment and disbelief at the ease with which we tolerate the iniquities of the present: the cruelty and pointless suffering which so besmirch our lives. Maitreya comes to do battle with this ancient wrong and to lead men into the Era of Light. Give Him your welcoming hand and let Him guide you to your Self. (*Share International*, July/August 2000)

This next article is called 'The Art of Living' and I will comment on it as we go on.

The Art of Living

by the Master –, through Benjamin Creme

Before long, a great change will take place in our approach to life. Out of the chaos of the present time will emerge a new understanding of the meaning underlying our existence and every effort will be made to express our awareness of that meaning in our daily lives. This will bring about a complete transformation of society: a new livingness will characterize our relationships and institutions; a new freedom and sense of joy will replace the present fear. Above all else, mankind will come to realize that living is an art, based on certain laws, requiring the function of the intuition for correct expression.

Harmlessness is the key to the new beauty in relationship which will emerge. A new sense of responsibility for actions and thoughts will guide each one in every situation; an understanding of the Law of Cause and Effect will transform men's approach to each other. A new and more harmonious interaction between men and nations will supplant the present competition and distrust. Gradually, mankind will learn the art of living, bringing to each moment the experience of the new. No longer will men live in fear – of the future and of each other. No longer will millions starve or carry the burden of labour for their brothers.

Each one has a part to play in the complex pattern being woven by humanity. Each contribution is uniquely valuable and necessary to the whole. However dim as yet the spark, there is no one in whom the fire of creativity cannot be lit. The art of living is the art of giving expression to that creative fire and so revealing the nature of men as potential Gods.

It is essential that all men share in this experience and learn the art of living. Until now, a truly creative life has been the privilege of the few; in this coming time the untapped creativity of millions will add a new lustre to the achievements of man. Emerging from the darkness of exploitation and fear, in true and correct relationship each man will find within himself the purpose and the joy of living.

The presence of the Christ and the Masters will speed this process, inspiring humanity to saner and safer methods of advance. A new simplicity will distinguish the coming civilization under the guidance of these Knowers of God.

Already, there is a growing sense that all is not well in man's estate. More and more, men are becoming aware of the limitations of their lives and search for something better. They question the modes and structures which inhibit participation in the fullness of life and long for meaning and purpose in all that they do.

Shortly, new energies will enter our lives and inspire men to creative action. A new and harmonious stimulus will be given to art and the art of living. A beauty not seen before will transform the ways of men and illumine for all time the nature of God.

Man stands now ready for Revelation. His heart and mind poised and turned to the future, he awaits the glory which, by readiness, he has invoked. (*Share International*, October 1983)

"Before long a great change will take place in our approach to life." It is already happening. There is already an undercurrent

of change, a simplifying of our demands on life, a growing distaste for materialism and all that it stands for across the world. As yet it is very fragmentary. There is no nation that one can point to which seems to be ahead of the others, as a whole, in carrying out this transformation.

Throughout this vast, complex country, the United States, there are pockets of thinkers and experimenters in living who are trying quite consciously to find the ways of the future. Looked at from this point they seem rather artificial. To use a well-honed esoteric word, they are filled with glamour, illusion. But the experiments are being made and a great deal is being learned. In this way the forerunners of the future are searching for the structures – political, economic, religious and social – which will characterize that future and make the present chaos a thing of the past.

We all know the chaos in which we live. There is nowhere in the whole of this world, with its 6.5 billion inhabitants, in which there is anything approaching harmony, right relationship. Harmony means right relationship.

Every painter and composer looks for harmony. It may seem disharmony to some, but to him, he is looking for harmony. He (or she) does so quite consciously to bring together into a whole the various parts that make up his piece of art – music or painting. He works until he has a sense that it is complete.

How does he know when it is complete? He knows little more about the painting or piece of music than the rest of us do. It is his or her piece of art, but until it is created, until it is a finished object, it is open to change. He has to come to a decision of when to stop. Something is driving him towards recognizing that moment of decision. It arrives when all the facets of the art are obeying the laws under which the art lives and expresses itself, and does so in a living, vibrating way.

There is no great joy to be had in creating dead art, although there is a great deal of dead art and music created. It may be that the work of art, conventional and dead, inert rhythmically, melodically and structurally, has nothing new to say, to give to the world. Being conventional, it will repeat more or less efficiently that which has been done before, perhaps thousands of times before. A copy, unless it is done with a certain quality, is already dead before it starts. There are great copies made by the artists themselves. I do not know if you can make a copy of music, but you can copy other people's style. Stravinsky was a master of reinventing old music, and used many scores by composers of the past to make something absolutely new – and also absolutely Stravinsky. That is the extraordinary thing, to take art of the past and make it entirely your own.

His friend Picasso did something very similar in painting. He could look at the art of the past and select from Velasquez, Manet, or some other artist whom he admired or envied. He could take art which sparked his creative act, to reinvent, using the forms, the ideas, the subject, the atmosphere of the original to create something altogether new.

That is how creativity works: by taking what is known and reinventing it all the way through. If you look at the painting of the past, listen to the music of the past, so different from the art and music of today, you recognize painters and musicians reinventing the past. They take their immediate forebears, learn from them, and add their individual voice to it.

Intuition

How do they do it? By what means can you put your voice, your own individuality into a painting or piece of music? It is not something you can buy in the shop and add on. It has to come from you. How do you decide when it works? Anyone can have the idea, but to have the idea and make that idea work so that a fragment of the art of the past becomes an art of the present day – new, fresh, interesting and never heard or seen before – requires something more.

It is done by the function and use of the intuition. Without intuition it could not happen, just as no creative art has ever been made without the function of the intuition. Since intuition is a soul quality, a demonstration of the soul working through its reflection – the man or woman who is composing or painting – it is the intuition, therefore, which is the creative fire behind the work of art. It comes from the soul. All the art and music of the past of quality – which stirs you, which lasts, has a meaning over hundreds, sometimes thousands, of years – is the demonstration of soul quality.

Art comes from the soul and is a demonstration through the intuition of the fact that men and women are souls. The more they act as souls, the higher the quality of art they will produce. It is always subject to the degree to which the soul has been able to demonstrate its creativity through the man or woman who is making the art. Art and culture come from the soul.

Without that knowledge of the soul, we build structures so that only a few people, relatively speaking, can in effect express the soul in their culture. We are all souls in fact, but we have to demonstrate that fact. If you are living in poorest Africa or parts of the world where there is only the meanest, basic kind of life, where for 18 hours a day you have to work just to feed yourself and your family, then, of course, there will be little or no art produced. The vehicles of the soul need leisure to enable the soul to demonstrate. The man or woman is the vehicle for the soul. If they have little or no leisure, they are not going to achieve a high demonstration of the creativity of the soul.

It is not that we need paintings or music to know that the soul exists, but since the soul does exist man has invented ways and means by which its expression takes place. Man loves to draw, to paint, to make music, to realize his instinct, his intuition of what is really the nature of life. He is expressing his response to life and the stimuli given to him in life. The better he does it, the more his soul is involved in the process. The more the soul is involved in the process, the deeper, more profound and the longer-lasting that art or music will be.

We can measure periods of time in which, as we look back historically, culture was at a high level and other periods when it was at a relatively low level. We can see thereby how the soul works cyclically through humanity. It takes a long time for humanity to evolve sufficiently to enable the soul to express itself. It is the soul in the man or woman that is expressing its awareness of the world of meaning. Above and beyond everyday experience, to the highest level of thought you can imagine, there is another level of being, the spiritual planes. That level of being gives to the person involved an awareness of the world of meaning. The world of the soul is the world of meaning.

The soul knows the meaning of life. It knows the purpose underlying our existence. It knows why we are here. We do not know why we are here. We do not know who we are, or our purpose. This is because we have allowed ourselves to be broken off from the source of our being which is the soul. We do not even know the human threefold constitution. We do not know that every man and woman is fundamentally a potential God.

We are sparks of the Divine, fragments of the Divine, with all of divinity inherent in that spark. Because of the nature of the world, of cosmos, the fact that one part is unseen but expresses itself in what we call life, the becoming, the evolution of life, makes the man or woman create on the outer physical plane, because that is where our vehicles live. This creates the conditions which are really coming through it from the soul level, if imperfectly.

Without the soul, the man or woman is nothing, if you can imagine a man or woman without a soul. The spark of God, the divine spark, reflects itself as a soul, and the soul reflects itself as the man or woman on the physical plane. The physical plane is tied to the spiritual planes by the fact of the soul. The soul acts as the divine intermediary between the spiritual plane, that which is not in matter, and matter itself, the physical plane. They are in polarity. The soul also fills the life and demonstrates the nature of the unseen aspect of man, the divine aspect, and describes that in its works, whether in science, music, painting, architecture or whatever. It expresses itself correctly above all, when it creates right relationship. It expresses itself incorrectly if the opposite results.

When we look around our world today, we see almost nothing but wrong relationships. If you have wrong relationships, you have conditioning. If you have conditioning, you have wars. All the wars, the suffering, the inability of humanity to demonstrate itself as souls in incarnation are the result of conditioning. Yet no one need be conditioned. Every single human being is conditioned – by the past, by its parents, by the very nature of its vehicles, which have been created for it by its soul under the Law of Karma. That great Law determines the physical nature, the emotional coloration and the mental factor of that individual. Karma brings it about and allows it to create right relationships in its short demonstration. We used to say 70 years, but it is a bit longer now. However short or long the life, it gives the person the opportunity to address the issues, to redress the wrongs done in the past and to resolve them, and therefore to make better human relationships in a particular life.

Reincarnation and Karma

We come into incarnation over and over again to enable us to right the wrongs of the past – our wrongs, not the wrongs of other people. Very few people in the West believe in reincarnation although a growing number of people accept it as an intellectual idea, possibly true. They do not quite know what it means, but they say: "Maybe in my last life I was a cat. That is why I like cats so much." That is the understanding of Western people on reincarnation. In the East millions of people have accepted reincarnation as part of the nature of their lives, but even they have not understood how that great Law works.

Life proceeds under law. Simple and obvious as it appears, it is something which has been left out of the equation. How many people, how many philosophers writing about the meaning and purpose of life, write about reincarnation as one of the laws, the Great Law of life? It is only in the esoteric teaching that the Law of Karma, the Law of Cause and Effect, is realized for what it is.

Jesus put it very simply: "As you sow, so shall you reap." It could not be put more simply, and you would think, more understandably. As you sow, whether in a cornfield or not, you will reap what you have sown. In good soil, with good seed (if you are lucky with the weather) then you get a good crop. If you sow bad seed and do not prepare the soil properly, you are going to get a poor crop. It is very simple. He put it that way because His audience were farmers and would know what He meant. But He is talking about the Law of Karma absolutely, clearly. He put it so neatly that nobody takes it very seriously, just one of those truisms which are not lived in practice.

The Law of Karma, the Law of Cause and Effect, is the Great Law governing all of our existence. Every thought, every action we make sets into motion a cause. The effects stemming from these causes make our lives for good or ill. We do it to ourselves. Because this Law substands the human condition on planet Earth, we are bound by it. There is nothing we can do about it except be harmless.

If you are harmless, you obey the Law. If you create right action, therefore, from right action can come only right reaction. But nine times out of ten, given the chance, humanity has created wrong action. We have always made wars. We have always stolen. We have always been greedy, selfish and complacent. All these actions which make up humanity's stock in trade are destructive. Hence the fact that we have a world that is destructive.

We have a world of earthquakes, floods, tsunamis and other catastrophes. We have air crashes, train crashes, car crashes and all the horrors of the physical plane. We know disease. We are killed by it. We are inhibited by it. We quickly age by it. Disease is a result of our wrong thought and action, and the wrong thought and action of our progenitors, because we inherit the tendency to one disease or another through our genetic framework.

So what can we do? It is obvious that we have to create harmlessness in every situation, in all relationships. When we create harmlessness in all relationships, we will find that the world is an easier, better, kinder, more harmonious place in which to live.

It seems so simple, but we find it incredibly difficult. It is so difficult to live in an artful way. I do not mean in an Artful Dodger way, but in a way that is graceful, elegant and meaningful, which obeys the laws of our nature, the fact that we are potential gods, ways which are filled with creativity. We are lucky if we have the leisure to become creative, but it needs leisure.

Most people today do not have the leisure. They may have the time, but time and leisure are not quite the same. They need the education, the instruction. They need the stimulus and the conditions in life of harmony, of harmlessness. They need to be eating at least once, preferably twice, a day, and to know where their food is coming from.

Unfortunately, there are millions of people in the world who do not have that pleasure, who hardly ever eat, who cannot remember when they last had a meal. Millions of people are dying in a world groaning with food. The world is so full of food that we do not know what to do with it. Sections of the world throw food away daily, and at the same time millions die for want of it. It is a terrible, painful situation – or should be painful. It is painful for the people who are neglected. It should be painful for all of us.

It should be a pain, a catastrophe in life to know that this continues daily, hourly, moment to moment. People are walking across deserts looking for aid agencies who, they have heard, are handing out food. Someone has said there is food being handed out, but eight days' trek across the desert if they can make it. They take their children and walk across the desert. This is the reality for millions of people. It should be so shocking, so painful, that we cannot stand it for one more day.

As the Master said, the time is coming when we will look back at this time absolutely unbelieving, unable to understand how we could do it. *"When in future times men look back to these climactic days they will wonder with astonishment and disbelief at the ease with which we tolerate the iniquities of the present, the cruelty and pointless suffering which so besmirch our lives."*

We take it so easily, even those of us concerned about it, who write and talk about it, join groups, and applaud the work of the non-governmental agencies who distribute food unceasingly. It is difficult to imagine how, as a race, we can put up with this state of affairs. "For how long," Maitreya says, "can you support this degradation?" It is a degradation of our life. It is a degradation of our reality as potential gods. We are so-called spiritual beings who do not demonstrate their

21

spirituality. We know it, but do not do it. We have not the will to do it.

Humanity in its present state is able to see the harm, the need, the horrors of today's world and shake their heads and give a donation to an aid agency. But we can quickly throw it off, unable to hold it and bring it to the point where the will takes over, so we can no longer stand that degradation. What is needed is the will of humanity aroused, not just its concern, to cleanse the world of these ills.

There are many more horrible iniquities in the world, terrible pain and suffering, disease and drug abuse. The use we make of other people, the unbelievable intolerance we have for other nationalities, other colours of men. We think that we are quite well-educated, well-evolved. Obviously we are not.

I believe it will take Maitreya to show humanity this iniquity, to show just how pressingly horrible it is. We all know it is horrible, but is it pressingly painful? Can we think about it with equanimity? If we can think about it with equanimity and it does not disturb us too much, then obviously we are not all that civilized, not all that evolved.

The Masters see humanity as having reached a point where they have the readiness to learn. That is why the Masters are here. We have invoked Them by being ready as never before to follow the precepts of the Masters and to create harmony and justice.

Equilibrium

It is harmony that the artist looks for, harmony that the composer seeks. The art might not look or sound all that harmonious, depending on the painter or composer, but he himself is seeking a point where he knows when he has created what for him is a harmony, a livingness, in the picture or music, when it obeys the laws of its nature, when it is complete, when he knows another stroke of the brush or another note would spoil it, would upset the equilibrium. He is all the time seeking equilibrium. He may not do it consciously but if he is a good painter or composer, he does it unconsciously. This sense of intuition guides him in the application of the colours and forms because there is nobody else. There is only his intuition to guide him. If he follows his intuition then he aims at completeness, and that completeness is unity. However unbalanced it might appear at first sight, he has to create an equilibrium. You do not create unity by bringing everything into a static condition. You can create unity by creating an unstatic condition and then bringing that into equilibrium. That equilibrium is the life of the picture or composition, or the life of the community in which you are working.

When humanity can create equilibrium in all aspects of its life, then we will know we are creating right human relationships. Right human relationships are harmless and in equilibrium. Equilibrium is balancing. There are many factors in life, and you have to bring them together, like many factors in a painting or sculpture. You have to create it in such a way that in the end you have created equilibrium, not a dead balance. In this way you create a living structure. If you want a harmony in colour you could paint it all one colour. But you want to give expression to many colours, many facets, many tones, and so you have to work harder, use your intuition to bring them all into a state of equilibrium. Equilibrium is not static.

Life is life when it is in equilibrium. When it is not in equilibrium, it is either destructive or static, on the point of dying. Static life is only static for a fraction of a second. The *status quo* is the last moment, but you are already out of the last moment. So there is no such thing as the *status quo*. There is always movement, and that movement is seeking stability. It is seeking unity, another word for equilibrium.

Likewise, all people are seeking unity. Underlying the search for meaning in the life of everybody is the search for unity. They want to be part of the group, of the human existence, because they are souls. They are already divine, and the nature of divinity is unity. There are countless millions of manifestations of that divinity in the universe, but the nature of the absolute divinity from which it all came is unified, unmoving, endless, eternal, never changing. That is behind each one of us. As Maitreya puts it, that is the Being of humanity. The becoming is what happens when that takes the form of living. We go through the process of evolution; that is the becoming. Essentially we are the Self, which is the Divine. Divinity, when we grasp it, when we understand it, recognize it, gives us the experience of what we call life. That is the meaning and essentially the purpose of who and what we are.

The following is another article by my Master.

The Laws and Rules of Life

by the Master –, through Benjamin Creme

Since time immemorial, men have known of, and expected the coming of, a great teacher, an outstanding man of wisdom and revealed truth. Cyclically, age after age, have these Great Ones come forth. Today is no exception to this cosmic law. As the new era dawns, men stand expectant as never before for a sight of the Great Teacher Who, though they know it not, is already in men's midst.

Throughout the planet, old and young, poor and rich, make ready for His Announcement, His Declaration of Mission and Purpose, His tryst with mankind. As the old century and era wind to their close, men's minds are quickening to the new energies which will fashion the forms of the new civilization and impose their qualities on the consciousness of men. These qualities – of synthesis and fusion, tolerance and goodwill, harmlessness and brotherly love – will, in time, bring the race of men to the manifestation of its destined glory. Thus shall it be, and thus shall men enter again into their age-old Covenant with the Divine.

Little though they may know it, men are on the threshold of a reawakening to the very meaning and purpose of their existence.

It is, in part, to see men safely through this period of trial and test that their Elder Brothers, the Masters of Wisdom, are returning openly to the world. With Their great leader – Maitreya, the World Teacher – at Their head, They will inspire the creation of the new, more appropriate structures which will allow men to live and work together in peace. From that peace will manifest a creativity and resource unlike aught seen before.

Men will learn and understand the subtle laws which govern their lives: the basic law of life, the Law of Karma, of Cause and Effect, which controls the destiny of all; the related Law of Rebirth, which makes possible the journey of the Soul in matter; the Law of Harmlessness, which governs right relationship, and the great Law of Sacrifice by which all evolution proceeds.

Through an understanding of these laws, men will come to resemble their Mentors, their Elder Brothers, and to demonstrate the Divinity shared by all. They will hearken to the teaching of the Wise Ones and, step by step, inherit their Birthright. Men are born to become Gods and nought can change that destiny; the timing, only, lies in men's hands.

Soon the world will know that the One for Whom men wait is now among us. Soon, indeed, will He show His face and beckon men to His side. Calling for justice for all will the

Great Lord stake His claim to the right to teach the Laws and Rules of Life, the Sacred Path by which men become Gods. (*Share International*, November 1999)

I have talked about the Law of Karma, the Law of Rebirth and the Law of Harmlessness, but the Law of Sacrifice is perhaps more difficult to understand. The great Law of Sacrifice is the very nature of evolution. We proceed in evolution through the sacrifice, always within ourselves, of the lower to the higher.

The soul's bodies of expression – physical, astral/emotional and mental – are vehicles. Maitreya calls them the 'temples' of the Self, through which the Self can see and watch the evolution of the soul in incarnation, the 'becoming' of ourselves as Gods. That process is done by refining the matter of the physical, astral/emotional, and mental equipment, refining them each life a little more, bringing into them more and more light, ie subatomic particles of matter. As the bodies gradually change, the nature and demands of the physical body change. Likewise, those of the astral/emotional body and finally of the mental body also change. Each change registers, for the Self watching this process, a shifting of status of a man or woman, coming into incarnation through the Laws of Karma and Rebirth, working under the Law of Harmlessness, and undergoing the process of the Law of Sacrifice. Each shift in the quality of energy of the physical, astral or mental bodies marks a degree of change which is a sacrifice because the lower is always sacrificed for the higher. Any evolutionary advance is achieved only through the sacrifice of some lower aspect. It is impossible to evolve and to remain the same at the same time.

We either advance and change or we do not advance. Every advance that we make is the result of a sacrifice of the lower: the desires and demands of the physical body, the attachments and desires of the emotional body, the conditioning of the mental body. The sense of the separated self has to disappear. When the ultimate demand – a complete sacrifice of the sense of self – happens, we are 'saved'. That is what salvation is, taking it out of a religious connotation. That is something which each of us has to do for ourselves. That is the ultimate goal of the evolution of humanity on this planet.

Then we are a Master. We are freed from this planet for ever. We are free from the pull of matter for ever. This bringing of light into the vehicle time after time is like dying to the past and being reborn to the future, the future being that which takes you along the evolutionary cycle to salvation or perfectionment. That is what perfectionment is, and it is always achieved by sacrifice. The great Law of Sacrifice is basic to the evolutionary process. That is hard for a lot of people to contemplate because they think sacrifice is something painful. But sacrifice of that kind 'happens'. You do not count the amount of light, subatomic particles, coming in, and say: "It is getting to a point where it is quite painful."

But you do realize in your life that things are never the same. You 'die' to what engaged your attention before. You 'die' to what was a need before. You 'die' to the demands of the physical body. You die to the demands and illusions of the astral body, to the paucity and narrowness of the mental body, because you are reaching higher and higher beyond these vehicles.

The soul is imbuing you with more and more subatomic particles, therefore light, and that is making you rarer. It is purifying, rarifying the vehicles of your body. The demands of the lower vehicles become less pronounced, and the demands of the soul become more pronounced. All you are doing really is replacing Earth light by soul light.

Matter is relatively inert and cumbersome, but, of course, you cannot work without it. You must go through evolution. It is something you need but are always refining. As you evolve, these vehicles are always being refined by more and more subatomic light, and that is the sacrifice. It is not really a sacrifice, but it is occultly a sacrifice. You sacrifice the lower matter to the higher light, and you eventually become a Master. Something we have to look forward to. Everybody in this room will become a Master – eventually.

We have to learn the art of living. It is an art form, and can only be learned as we go. It is not something that you can teach, but you can teach the rudiments, the laws. Teach the laws and the rules which stem from them – the Law of Cause and Effect, the Law of Rebirth, the Law of Harmlessness and the Law of Sacrifice – and you have taught the basics of life. Life proceeds under these Laws, and the sooner we make them instinctive parts of our life the sooner we will have a reasonably co-ordinated and harmonic life and world. It is a world filled today with anxiety and fear. The nature of life should be the very opposite. One day, with the help of Maitreya and the Masters, it will be so.

Coming into the world relatively soon is the great 4th ray, the Ray of Harmony through Conflict. We know plenty about the conflict; we are going through the conflict. The 4th Ray of Harmony controls the human Kingdom. It is the governing ray of humanity. By its nature it creates the conditions necessary for fast human evolution: conflict, and for harmony as a result of that conflict.

That great ray is always in manifestation as far as humanity is concerned, but in a few years from now it will enter a major cycle and will stimulate all life on the planet to an extraordinary degree. Also coming in is the great 7th ray under the Aquarian dispensation. This combination of 4 and 7 is unique. It is wonderful. It supplies all that we need in the form of harmony and structure.

The Master DK has written (through Alice A. Bailey): "Artists are to be found on all the rays, but the combination of

4 and 7 makes for the highest type of artist." You can see this by an examination of the ray structures of some of the great artists of the past. Leonardo da Vinci has only 4 and 7 except for one little random 3 that got in somehow. You can see the kind of artist he was in all fields.

This combination of 4 and 7 will have a tremendous impact on humanity. The 7th ray grounds the spiritual ideal. It anchors on the physical plane the energy of synthesis pouring in from Aquarius through Maitreya, Who will focus it into the world. This will have a colossal impact, is already having an impact, drawing people together, drawing nations together. These powerful cosmic forces are doing their work and will continue to do their work. They will draw humanity into a synthesis, a blended, fused oneness. People will know the unity they are searching for because the nature of that oneness is unity. They will have true equilibrium. The combination of 4 and 7 (if it is about 50/50) creates the kind of equilibrium I have been talking about in terms of an art form.

We are all seeking balance. We are seeking unity, equilibrium, however we define it. It is that which allows us to be creative and happy. It allows the wheel to turn again and again, and create out of itself, and again out of itself, that which is created. In that way the civilization of the future will demonstrate qualities we cannot even begin to talk about. We do not have words for what we will see and know. We do not have words for the quality of that civilization. Nor for the feeling, the experience, of that relationship when all people see and experience themselves as brothers and sisters of one home, one planet. That will take people back to the experience of childhood. Home was home. Your brothers and sisters were the staff that kept you on the right track. So it will be.

We will truly depend on each other. An interdependent world will be a reality. It is today a reality, but we do not recognize the fact. In this coming time the constructions, the inventions, the extraordinary discoveries latent yet just beyond us at the present moment will become realities. We will unleash them through correct relationship, leisure, education, recognition in the world for the first time that we are souls in incarnation on a journey of exploration together, creating the artefacts of that civilization and demonstrating that we are Gods.

What it really means is that we together as a people, a group called humanity, will give expression to our inner reality as Gods. The soul will express itself. The Self, through our life, will envelop all people. We will see all people as the soul. We will see that there is only one Self, and that we all share identity with that Self. Maitreya is here to help us to see that, to teach us how to become that which we are.

I am going to finish by reading a few of the sayings of Maitreya. One could go on indefinitely because they are such a rich mine of truth, unbelievable knowledge and wisdom.

Maitreya's Teachings on Awareness

Below are sayings taken from *Maitreya's Teachings: The Laws of Life*. Maitreya is talking about new awareness.

"The light, the bible, the prayer for one and all from now on, is the awareness that Maitreya is in you and you are in Him. His vibrant teachings are stirring the world now, and the politicians are silent."

Maitreya is the embodiment of the Christ Principle, the energy of love. As the Christ Principle is awakened where it is not yet awakened, and stimulated where it is awakened, it will transform the world. In that sense Maitreya can say: *"I am with you and in you. I seek to express that which I am through you. For this I come.* " He says that that is the new Bible, the new light, the new prayer for one and all from now on. Know that Maitreya is within you, that you are in Him.

Nothing which we do is unseen and unheard and has no response from Him. Every vibration of love that we send out finds its response in the heart of Maitreya. He is the embodiment of the consciousness aspect of humanity. It is through consciousness and development of conscious awareness that we evolve. In that way He stimulates our awareness, our consciousness. The more we are aware of Him in us and us in Him, the surer we are on our path and the more we can give to those around us.

He says: *"Your destiny is freedom. No one is 'born in sin'. Rather, the Self is subject to conditioning during the process of evolution. The process of evolution is the Becoming."*

Through the process of evolution, of becoming that which we already are potentially, in essence as the Self, conditioning sets in.

"If you follow the three principles of honesty of mind, sincerity of spirit and detachment, evolution proceeds naturally. Your 'second nature' is conditioned nature, but practice of the three principles will free you from conditioning. No one is 'condemned' to conditioning.

"Do not cheat yourself. Respect yourself.

"What is peace? 'In creation, peace means non-conditioning. What is war? War means conditioning.'"

Maitreya says many spiritual teachers, gurus and saints reach a point of awareness and then stick there. They personify. They see that wisdom, that knowledge, that experience as themselves. It is not them. It is an experience, not them personified. By personifying it they lose the ability to evolve further, to become what they are essentially.

"This time," Maitreya says, *"I Myself have come. I cannot be caught in any isms."*

If you teach that which you discover, you create an 'ism' – Buddhism, Christianity, Islam, Judaism, Hinduism. These are all isms. They are all created by learned men who experienced and then stopped. They did not go beyond the experience of that knowledge of what they called divinity, which is a structure around their awareness of divinity. *"'I, Myself, have come. I cannot be caught in any isms.'* The time will come when people will understand this naturally without fuss because they feel free within. This is why Maitreya says: *'I have not come to create followers.'"*

If you follow Maitreya in the sense that you would follow Mohammed, Jesus or the Buddha, you are creating a coercion in yourself. You are no longer yourself. You are a follower. It is not interesting to be a follower. It is not that Christianity, Buddhism or Hinduism is wrong or not right, it is that they are not you. If you follow, you are losing yourself. You have to be who you are. Hinduism, Buddhism or Christianity might help you to come to know who you are, but it is the knowing who you are that is the important thing, not being a follower of Buddha, Krishna or Jesus.

Maitreya says: *"Religion is like a ladder. It can help you to get onto the roof. But once you are on the roof you do not need it."* You can give the ladder to somebody else or throw it away. It is not right to follow anybody, not even Maitreya. He says: *"I have not come to create followers."* He does not want you to follow Him. He wants you to find out who you are and to be who you are. It cannot be separate from Him because He already knows who you are. He is already in you because He is the embodiment of the consciousness aspect of humanity. That is why He is the Christ. That is what the Christ is. But to follow Him means to negate yourself by putting a religion around Him. He is not asking you to follow His religion. He is not selling a religion.

"I have not come to create followers. What is important is your Self, free from compulsions, able to fulfil your duty without a sense of burden, not bothered by praise or criticism."

"The moment you feel divinity within you, you realize that everything is within you. The master key is within you. If you have a direct experience of the Lord, that is the Almighty, Divinity, will it matter, then, whether you become a millionaire, a king or a beggar?

"This experience alone is sufficient to create equilibrium in mind, spirit and body. This experience can never change. It is eternal. When you experience the Almighty, you do not create divisions."

"Be what you are. Do not follow one another."

I have asked people: "Do you believe in this story of mine?" Some say: "Well, I do not know. I would rather ask some of my friends what they think." As if they could get something more from their friends about what I am saying than they were getting from me, there and then. I say: "How could they tell you? They do not know. So how could that benefit you?" They had not thought of that, but they feel they have to ask, see how their friends are reacting to it. If their friends are reacting to it well, positively, then the chances are they do the same. Why? Because they are just copying their friends. It is copying and that is how some people think, respond to life. They say: "How do my friends do it? Which pictures do my friends like? I like those too. What music do my friends like? Me too. That is why they are my friends because we all like the same music. We all like the same paintings, the same food."

We do not have to be like our friends. Maitreya says no two people are alike. You cannot make a carbon copy of any two people in the world. We are each of us entirely unique. We have the same needs, more or less, but we are different. We each have a unique thing to give to the world.

No one can be an exact copy of anybody else, so why try? The interest of you to your friends is that you are different; you are unique. And to God, to that from which we all come, He took infinite trouble in making these sparks all different. He sends them down through all the planes until they come onto the physical plane, and then by ship to America!

We should not try to copy each other. We should not try to be the same person. Everybody is needed by God, no less, to be exactly who they are. That is why He made us under all these different ray structures. Why do we have all the different ray structures? Because they are needed. These rays of souls and monads are needed by God for His plans. He has plans, but He is not going to do it. We have to do it, because we are God. Essentially we are God and have to carry out the plans of the Old Man.

If we copy other people, we are not ourselves. He made us unique. We may be a 'common working chap', but we have a job to do – that is, become a God.

"Be what you are. Do not follow one another. Gradually you will become evolved. No two persons are alike. No two persons can be carbon copies. The moment you take on another's personality you are creating a distance between Me and you. The moment you are what you are, you begin to enjoy bliss, serenity, tranquillity. Then there is no distance between us.

"I am the nectar. I am the poison. The moment you realize you are not mind, spirit and body, not even the life force, that is immortality. At that stage you can take charge of your own destiny. You are a spark of the Almighty."

"I am with you and with everyone. I never give up anyone."

"The truth has many faces, but the main chord is within the individual. The moment you feel Oneness, when you speak, the basic chord of truth sings within. Experience Me. Be what you are. The moment you try to be what you are, you experience who you are, why you are."

"People respond. But if you try to twist the truth or to make money out of it, it becomes so distorted that people begin to lose interest in it."

THE ART OF LIVING

QUESTIONS AND ANSWERS

Edited version of the Question and Answer session with Benjamin Creme from the 2005 Transmission Meditation Conferences held in San Francisco, USA, and Kerkrade, the Netherlands.

THE LAW OF KARMA, THE LAW OF HARMLESSNESS

Would you please give a few examples of how we might make best use of the Law of Karma?

The best way is to be harmless in every situation. Most people will be harmless in one situation and harmful in another. There are very few people (they must be saints if they exist) – apart from the Masters, Who are saints – who are harmless in every situation. Because of our glamours, our conditioning, inevitably we are harmful in some situations, less harmful in others, perhaps not at all harmful in others, but in enough to create our karma. The answer is very simple, although difficult. Like everything, it requires discipline.

To be harmless in every single situation – think of the control that one needs. Control can be made easier by meditation and by the positive, definite function of the will to be harmless in as many situations as we recognize. We will be harmful in many situations and not even recognize the fact; I am sure this happens all the time. It is only afterwards that we realize how harmful we have been.

I am sure, for instance, that Mr Bush is a sincere Christian. Yet look at the harm he did in Afghanistan, at the harm he has done in Iraq. The harm he and those around him are doing to the liberty of the American people right now, thinking up ways and means of curtailing their liberty. All of us have the illusion that we are harmless. We know the length to which we would not go, but anything up to that, if it is necessary, is acceptable. We are often harmful, knowing that we are harmful, but not appreciating the depth of the harm, and able, because of our glamours, to rationalize it away altogether.

It always mystifies me how some people I have met, so versed in the Alice Bailey teachings that they actually lecture on them, have said to me: "I go along with everything you say about the coming of the Hierarchy and Maitreya and so on, but what I am unable to take is this idea you have of sharing the resources of the world." It staggers me. I do not know what they have been reading, or how they have read what DK says about the sharing of resources. It is one of the main subjects in the *Problems of Humanity* (by Alice A. Bailey).

This belief is held in all seriousness. "We do not have much, but what we have is ours. We have worked hard all our lives for what we have," (living in one of the better parts of Southern California, on the beach!) "I do not see how we need to share what we have with people that we do not even know." "They might have long hair or Rastafarian haircuts!" Or "Why do they (the starving millions of Africa) not lift themselves up by the bootstraps as we have done?" That is how we hoodwink ourselves, how we put this glamour over the reality that we do not want to see. We are able to exclude it nicely, find some rationalization for it.

If you want to, you can rationalize anything. You should hear Mr Blair rationalizing why Britain went to war in Iraq, why it was not something he had to apologize for (and has never apologized for) even though 70 per cent of the British people were against it. The advice from all the best minds in Britain were against it, not to mention the French, Germans and the other Europeans.

It is the easiest thing in the world to rationalize. Certain rays, and certain kinds of minds, therefore, make it easier to rationalize away the things that are uncomfortable. They are uncomfortable if you see them. But you can rationalize them away, put them behind you and 'steer forward into the future' like Mr Blair and Mr Bush are doing. They want you to forget their mistakes and see only what they tell you are the possibilities ahead. All governments do it. They have done so from time immemorial, and will go on doing it, given the chance. It is up to us to not give them the chance.

I thought that harmlessness was not hurting others, but it must be much more. Would you please give a few examples of the best use of harmlessness?

It means not waging war even if you want to. It means not toppling governmental heads, especially if they are democratically chosen by the people, as Allende was in Chile but was toppled by the CIA. You should not do that. That is harmful. It is done by governments who overreach themselves, overestimate their power and, therefore, the right to do whatever they want. They want to keep spheres of influence free from communism or any other nasty thing that they imagine, and so control the ground all around them. All these big dominating powers do the same thing. They want an area around them that makes them feel safe. They control the economies of the nations around them. The US sees Canada, Mexico, Brazil and all other South American nations in that light. If a leader comes to the fore who has socialistic tendencies, the US government quickly gets the CIA to do the dirty job which it is not prepared to do in public. That is what happens at governmental levels throughout the world. They are fascist, more or less.

The best use of harmlessness is to do the opposite of that, to build ties, share resources, and work co-operatively with other nations. Co-operation is harmless. Lack of co-operation, which is competition, is in its very nature harmful. Yet every young American is brought up to believe that competition is the wellspring of life itself. It is not. It is harmful and degrading to the human spirit. It is corrupting and divisive, and the opposite, therefore, of harmless, incurring thereby the Law of Karma.

The karma of some of these leaders is not to be forgotten – Mr Bush and Mr Blair and all the tyrants down the ages, including Saddam Hussein. They are tyrants in one way or another. They seek power and misuse it.

Jesus said: "As you sow, so shall you reap," speaking of the Law of Karma. How do we help ourselves and others see that Law working out in our lives? For example, why has George Bush's karma not caught up with him?

You are impatient. It is coming, believe me!

Let me give illustrations. Say America goes to war then there are floods, hurricanes, tornadoes, and unbelievable weather, 150 degrees in the shade over America for weeks on end. There is drought. People die in the hundreds from the heat. That is the Law of Karma.

Read the new book, *The Laws of Life*, by Maitreya. He uses a lot of illustrations showing the actions of nations in the world and the repercussions which we do not even see – the earthquakes, tornadoes, floods, volcanic eruptions, air crashes, train crashes, all of which are karmically induced by the disequilibrium which we have created.

Whenever you violate the Law of Karma you upset the equilibrium of the world to some extent. Depending on the size of the action, the repercussions may be trivial or enormous.

With actions like an attack on Iraq, the repercussions are enormous. When millions of people are filled with the same harmful thought, and it is carried out, the karmic effect is likewise enormous.

When you call somebody a bad name, a liar, a cheat, a so-and-so, these are little violations of the karmic law.

What is the most important thing to avoid bad karma?

If we obey the laws, work and live within the laws, if we obey the law of harmlessness, we automatically work with the beneficent Law of Karma. We do not create bad karma because we are harmless.

The Masters do not create any personal karma because They are absolutely harmless. They have to work within the Law of Karma as it affects the world, our karma, but they cannot create wrong karma Themselves. That is what we should aim at, and is how we control our karma. It is a law, but you can work with the law or against the law. You are either legal or illegal. If you are illegal, you suffer, make bad karma. You are put in the prison of your mind and heart.

CONFLICT RESOLUTION

How can we resolve conflicts harmlessly?

There is not one way to solve conflicts harmlessly. There is a way which if followed will eventually work out and, in the most harmless way, resolve to the greatest extent the conflicts and that is to accept that you need to give in order to receive.

If you have two people, and you have a conflict which involves both of you, say a conflict about land or water or oil, for example, how do you do it? You meet with the other side and seek a compromise, something that satisfies you both. It will not be all that you, from your position, would hope to gain but, by giving a certain amount, not demanding the full 100 per cent of your rights, and your opponents also approaching it in the same harmless way, sacrificing again some of their rights, you reach a compromise.

By using wisdom, wise compromise, you arrive at an acceptable agreement and so keep the peace or end the conflict without any further harm.

How does the time element tie into harmlessness?

If it is like the Israelis and the Palestinians, you meet endlessly for years and the Palestinians make some compromise and the Israelis say: "No, it is not acceptable." Then the Israelis offer a tiny, miniscule compromise, something that is practically meaningless and, of course, the Palestinians reject it outright. And then the Israelis say: "You see, they do not accept what we offer." And so the fighting goes on. You have to do it with truth. You have to be honest in what you are doing. For one thing, you have to want the aimed-at result.

In the Palestinian/Israeli situation, the Israelis obviously do not want the peace. They want peace, but not at the expense of giving up the West Bank. The West Bank was negotiated for the Palestinians by Maitreya with the King of Jordan in April 1991, at a Conference of leaders in all fields hosted by Maitreya in London. Maitreya asked King Hussein if he would give up sovereignty of the West Bank, which has been in the hands of the Israelis since the Six Day War of 1967. King Hussein agreed on condition that it became a homeland for the Palestinian people. The Israelis have never had any intention of giving up the whole of the West Bank. And there are Israelis, not all Israelis, but a large minority, who are sworn never to give up the West Bank, the land of Canaan which, as far as they are concerned, was granted them by God thousands of years ago. The Palestinians, for their part, have a minority who have sworn to resist the presence of Israel in the land which has been theirs for centuries. And so you have fanatics on both sides who will never give in, and you have to aim at a compromise which will bring a just peace. Personally, I think only Maitreya can end the Israeli/Palestinian situation with an agreeable compromise, with the Palestinians accepting the existence of Israel, and the Israelis accepting the right of the Palestinians to the West Bank and a just and viable independent state.

How does the time element tie in? In the Palestinian/Israeli situation you can see how time is very important. It drags on and on with no resolution. It changes its focus. People, like President Arafat, die; the King of Jordan died and that changes the situation. The Israelis and the Americans think they can take advantage of the situation because they have sidelined Mr Arafat. The Palestinians no longer have a leader, and so it is thought they will be more amenable to accepting the injustice which has been offered them to date. Until there is an acceptable and just compromise there will be no end to warfare there.

So the time factor is meaningful – it usually is. Everything that happens on Earth has already happened on the higher planes. It happened out of time, from our point of view, maybe many years ago. From the point of view of timelessness in which the Masters work it is not a case of 'many years ago' or 'in many years to come'. It is now, because from Their experience, there is only now. There is no future and no past. This is life now at this very moment. But to precipitate onto the physical plane takes 'time' – in that relative sense of time that we use from our physical-plane consciousness. When we have to catch a flight we get to the airport two hours beforehand in order to catch it. If we did not, if we just turned up – "I feel that the time has arrived" – the plane would be gone. We would be left stranded, waving goodbye.

We need this time arrangement on the physical plane because it is precipitated at last onto the physical plane and is an event. If we make relationships depending on these events in time, then of course time is involved and must be taken account of. And as Shakespeare put it, "There is a tide in the affairs of men, which, if taken at the flood. . ."; you get what is accruing outside time, ready to happen. The happening is the precipitation onto the physical plane of the results of thoughts already registering on the higher planes. These are plans, thoughts and constructions of the minds of men – to some extent, but of Masters from a much higher level and of the Will of the Logos of our planet. So they are the result of karma, the results of events which we have set in motion from our previous actions or thoughts, which might be good or bad.

The Masters say that we make more good karma than bad karma. I know it does not feel like that, but that is what is said. When the thoughts and plans precipitate, we call that an event, a happening, a tsunami, or a hurricane that invades our coastland and causes devastation and death. All of that is set in motion on the higher planes by the actions of the devic elementals which are in charge of the forces of nature. They regulate the climate and so on. They are responding to the upheaval, the tensions created by men.

What can we do as individuals to resolve the conflict between more control from above and the need for leisure?

By "above", I suppose you mean the office manager, your boss, and the need for leisure? You have to work that out for yourself. You have to change the government. You have to start with your little group of would-be dictators who are running your individual countries. The people everywhere have to assert their need for leisure.

How can I be harmless within my own state of conflict?

It is more difficult if one thinks of oneself as full of conflict. And, of course, we are all involved in conflict. And you cannot be harmless in a state of conflict. It is precisely in a state of conflict that we produce the actions which are harmful.

If we are not in conflict we are in harmony. If we are in harmony, we do not produce harm because harmony produces that state of inner relaxation and lack of conflict that produces no wrong action. As soon as we are in conflict then the potential for harm is increased, inevitably.

So: "How can I be harmless within my own state of conflict?" Well, you cannot, except by resolving the conflict. You cannot deal with the harm until you are able to deal with the conflict. If you deal with the conflict in yourself and produce harmony instead of conflict then you will find the harm ceases. You stop being harmful.

HARMLESSNESS AND HARMFULNESS

Can you say more about harmlessness and harmfulness? For example, how do we practise harmlessness? Is it to do with intention?

The best way to practise harmlessness is to practise detachment. The more detached you are, the more harmless you will be.

The Masters say that the Law of Karma is a beneficent law and generally we have more good karma than bad karma. Some people find that hard to believe, but that may be just self-pity. So practise.

"Is it to do with intention?" Of course, it is to do with intention.

When we catch ourselves having a harmful thought, what is the best way to change it? Some people cancel the thought. Some surround it in the light to be transformed. How can it be changed to be harmless?

Do not say it. If you catch yourself having a harmful thought, take it back. Say: "Oh no. Slipped there!" Get your mind in sync again and lift your attention up. If you take your attention to the ajna centre, you are not going to have a harmful thought. All your harmful thoughts are coming from the solar plexus. Who has not had a harmful thought? Harmful thoughts go through our minds all the time. We simply take them back. Say: "Well, I did it again. I must watch it." There is no easy way. If there were, we would all be harmless. The real answer is to be detached.

Can true forgiving wipe out some harm?

True forgiving can do wonders, but who is to do the forgiving? If you cause harm to someone and, of course, they are aware of it, they feel it, and they know who did the harm, and they forgive you for your action, they mitigate the action of karma in the degree to which they truly forgive. If the forgiveness is total, if they are so detached that they can completely, sincerely, deeply forgive totally the harm done against them – and it is quite difficult for any human being under a certain degree to do that – then they can wipe out the karma involved in your harmful action. And, of course, you can do the same in a similar situation to the degree that you are detached. To the degree that detachment allows you to forgive then it mitigates the karma involved.

If it is total, like the forgiveness of Jesus, for instance, Who was a fourth-degree initiate at the time, it is total. As He said on the cross: "Forgive them Father, for they know not what they do." That coming from Him and from His detachment is total.

But if a person says: "Oh, it is all right. Forget it. I forgive you, you so-and-so," then the karma is only partially removed, and it is difficult for people to be totally forgiving because it is difficult for people to be totally detached.

We have to be detached to be able to forgive. If we are detached enough, then we can forgive and be untouched by the harm, and, therefore, it can mitigate the karma involved for the harming person.

THE LAW OF SACRIFICE

Could you elaborate on the connection between the Law of Harmlessness and the Law of Sacrifice?

We live in an energetic universe, we are all vibrating. The process of living is a process by which the vehicles, physical, astral, mental, gradually change their nature. It is very practical.

If you want to live in a higher sphere – that is, in a sphere in which your mind can be attuned to a higher level of the meaning and purpose of our existence in the world – then you have to have vehicles which allow that to take place. You cannot bring into a mental vehicle that for which it is not yet attuned to grasp. So it has to be vibrating at finer levels. You refine the vehicles. You refine the physical vehicle by all sorts of ways which people call self-sacrifice: diet, fasting, exercise. They might walk or run, or they might go on a bicycle, even if the bicycle is not moving. They do not get anywhere, but they are still cycling away. They are hot, sweating and they are elevated physically. They are refined. They do this every day for 10 years or half a lifetime and gradually it refines the physical body.

Then through life they refine the astral/emotional body and then, eventually, the mental body. Each of them goes through a process of refinement, and that allows the vehicles to attract to themselves more and more light, more and more matter of subatomic nature, and that transforms the person. That is where the sacrifice comes in. They have to leave that matter behind and go on.

Is there any relationship between an individual's sacrifice and the underlying Law of Sacrifice?

I am talking about occult sacrifice, not being asked to carry a bomb and blow yourself up with it, which is not an occult sacrifice, but meaning the Law of Sacrifice in the occult sense, the renunciation of the lower for the higher. Then, of course, there is a direct relationship.

The personal, individual change that brings about the action of the Law of Sacrifice, and the change that takes place as a result of that, are to do with the Law of Sacrifice. They change you.

The Law of Sacrifice is an action from an occult point of view. You are changing yourself. You do not go back to where you were. That is the past, and you are changing the past for the future. You are changing yourself from what you were to what you are potentially. So every act of sacrifice under the Law of Sacrifice is changing the potential you into the real you. You are you, but in potential. Through action on yourself, you invoke the Law of Sacrifice.

The Law of Sacrifice ensures that you renounce the past and in so doing can achieve the results of the sacrifice which is invoked by the need to advance. It is the law of evolution which is driving you onward. Your aspiration acts through the law of evolution which draws from you the sacrifice needed to reach a higher state.

That aspiration is the law of evolution. We experience it as aspiration. So we create, eventually, we grow the qualities that we attract from the aspiration, the qualities that bring that aspiration about.

Can you elaborate more on the Law of Sacrifice. How does it work?

As a person grows, aspiration draws him/her higher and higher and when the higher is attainable you find that it is only attainable through sacrifice.

You have to sacrifice that which you no longer need even if you have needed it all your life to that point. It is no longer of use to you in the higher vibrational state in which you now are. If you sacrifice the lower, you sacrifice the vibrational state of the lower for the higher vibrational state.

Every time your vibrational life is enhanced and you go up a notch in vibration, you draw to the bodies, physical, astral and mental, subatomic energy, which is light, so that the bodies are transformed gradually. You cannot keep the lower vibrating matter which is now being turned into light. You cannot have the lower vibration coexisting with the higher vibration.

It is so simple really. It obeys a natural law. There is nothing mystical about it. If you do something which takes you to a higher level, you are changing the vibrational rate, therefore, you cannot keep that which is still vibrating at a lower rate. You have to give it up, sacrifice it.

If you are making a change in the vibrational nature of your vehicles, you can only do so by getting rid of the lower vibrational rate that they were before. So that lower matter has to go back into the matter of the universe, the life of the planet in which we live. You cannot take it with you.

Could you speak about the link between the will and the Law of Sacrifice, and the importance of implementing the will in the art of living?

You cannot carry out the Law of Sacrifice without the will. There has to be a willing surrender of the lower for the higher.

It is not about self-sacrifice. Some rays, the 6th ray in particular, have the function of self-sacrifice as a major aspect of their quality on the soul level. That is behind the tremendous sacrifice of Jesus. But sacrifice as a principle in the art of living is actually the recognition of sacrifice as an intrinsic part of the path of evolution. You cannot evolve along the evolutionary path without sacrifice, without having the will to give up the lower for the higher.

It does not always entail a conscious effort of will, but it is always a willed process. But the will does not strongly come into the process until the third initiation is taken. Then the will takes a very powerful part in the further advance of the disciple. But until that point the ability to sacrifice is the ability to surrender the lower – that which is less valuable and needs transcending – for that which is yet to be realized. That should be a natural part of the art of living.

There can be a desire to sacrifice. This often brings the benefits, the blessings of the Masters and of Deity itself. The instinct to sacrifice is the unconscious instinct to let die that which is dying, to give it up.

Very often we hold on to something for which we have no further use. It is not really part of our life equipment. We have done it, we have been through it, and we should never try to hold on to and personify it. If we hold on to it, we personify it. We make it ours. We think: "I have achieved!" If you do that, you make no further progress. If you do that with Maitreya, you weaken Maitreya's life in you. You should not, and He will not, be personified. That is why He does not want followers. If you personify Him, you make Him the head of a religion. He is not and has no intention of becoming that. He has a role to play. He is an initiator, He is a teacher, but He will not be personified.

If you do that to yourself, if you make an advance to a certain point, you have to be prepared to give up that which you gained because it is already part of you. Many personify. They say: "I have attained that, and I have done that. I think I am coming near the such and such initiation." It is a glamour. What you are really doing is conditioning yourself by personifying yourself. You should not measure it. You should not personify. It is simply an area of activity which you reach, give to, learn from, give up, and go on higher and yet higher.

In the evolutionary process you go from physical-plane consciousness to soul consciousness. That is a journey. If you have astral consciousness, the consciousness of the physical plane drops below the level of thought. It becomes subconscious, instinctive. We do not go about being conscious of the physical plane. We do it automatically. We say automatically, but it is subliminal. It is subconscious. The astral activity should be below the level of thought, but it galvanizes and stimulates our actions. It is nothing to do with that. That is not the function of the astral plane.

The astral plane should really be a still, undisturbed mirror, like a pond. On that pond, the consciousness of buddhi, which is soul consciousness, should be reflected as intuition. But how many people's astral body is the reflection of buddhi?

We can know anything from the intuition, but only if the intuition is contactable. As soon as you give a name to anything achieved, as soon as you identify with that achievement and hold on to it, you personify it. That is what it is like to personify. We have to go beyond that to a higher level, from physical consciousness to astral consciousness to mental consciousness to spiritual consciousness. That is a progression, and we have to do it. That is the only way we can advance.

That is where the sacrifice comes in. It is not sacrifice of the self for the planet. It is a sacrifice for the soul for the planet that it comes into incarnation and takes on these vehicles. But the vehicles on the return journey have to be sacrificed one by one. The physical-plane consciousness has to be sacrificed. It does not go away. It just has not to be the top of your achievement. Likewise, the astral, mental and three levels of the spiritual. The ones below all have to be superseded, otherwise there is no progress if you are holding on to each step of the way. Maitreya cites certain gurus, saints, holy men, who have achieved a certain level and then personify it and remain at that level. They identify with their experiences, achievement and personify it, thinking they are now enlightened.

There is an ancient conditioning that thinks suffering is sacrificing. Through the religious traditions we have been led to believe that the more we suffer, the more we sacrifice and vice versa. Though practise of the Art of Living involves pain at times, sacrifice of the lower for the higher involves joy of the soul.

This is true. There is a long-standing religious tradition, especially in the devotional religions like Christianity and Islam, which equates sacrifice with the end of suffering, but entailing suffering. That entails suffering as the ultimate sacrifice, that the more we suffer, the more we sacrifice.

Underlying the devotional attitudes of Christianity and Islam is the idea of sacrifice; they mistake the role of sacrifice, of the Law of Sacrifice. But they have got an inkling of it, and it is seen as the method *par excellence* of overcoming the ego. They have recognized that the ego must be overcome and to go beyond the ego and to become totally detached. The way to do it is by making oneself suffer, which has two roles in the Christian tradition. One is the coming close to Jesus because He suffered so much from the flails of the scourges which were used on Him before the crucifixion. By doing the same thing on oneself, the idea is, one recognizes, appreciates, comes close to, if the mind and heart are aligned in this, the suffering of Jesus. There is no doubt that that can be a way, a mode of procedure, for some religious people.

They have recognized that the quality inherent in the 6th ray at the soul level (and both Christianity and Islam are 6th ray religions) is the reality of sacrifice. It is as if they have recognized the esoteric meaning of the 6th ray instinctively, intuitively, through the sacrifice of Jesus. He demonstrated the supreme sacrifice to illustrate that experience, and many have gone a similar way and have reached Mastery through that same spirit of self-sacrifice.

It is sacrificing the lower man for the higher man all the time. It is writ large in the qualities of the 6th-ray soul, that the method *par excellence* is the path of sacrifice. That does not mean that everything on the physical plane that is difficult, nasty, smelly, unpleasant and tiring to do should be taken on by the devotee. But there are those on that path who are put through precisely the taking on of the worst possible conditions in order to overcome the ego. It is basically all about overcoming the ego and approaching the reality of the soul. That is what sacrifice is.

I speak as an esotericist and put it in a different way – the overcoming of the lesser for the higher. The lesser way, the path of the man, the reality of his physical body, his astral/emotional body, his mental body. The soul does not have these. That is why the man has them. We have them to enable the soul to use them, to see this physical-plane reality, which is the process of conditioning.

Disciples, those who are disciplining themselves, have to make their return journey and sacrifice their experience of the physical, the astral/emotional and the mental planes in order to reach the spiritual synthesis of the soul. That is why sacrifice is a way.

This can be individual glamour and illusion, in part, but nevertheless basic to both Christianity and Islam is this concept of sacrifice, meaning it in its highest level. Of course, today Islam distorts it. Those imams, and those who would have the young becoming 'martyrs', train the young to sacrifice themselves in order to 'meet their maker' and to earn their poor families some extra money. They are then able to blow themselves up. That is the ultimate sacrifice, but it does not make them something they were not before.

If they were conditioned and filled with illusion, which I am sure mainly they were, then they remain that, and they come back into incarnation at the same stage as they were. So they have made that ultimate sacrifice for nothing, simply to carry out the plans of some fanatical group.

There is, therefore, suffering that is useless. One of the roles of Maitreya is precisely to free humanity from unnecessary suffering. We all allow ourselves to suffer unnecessarily because we take the astral plane as real. We take our astral life as real life. We take our conditioning as a normal condition. None of that is true. It is unnecessary suffering, which we put ourselves through and is the opposite of freedom. Religious groups, too, have given humanity an enormous weight of unnecessary guilt. There is a core to the Christian and the Islamic tradition in which suffering rightly is seen as a means, as a path, and that in suffering you relate more correctly to other people.

What is wrong with most political leaders in the West today is that so often they have never known what it is like to lack anything. They are usually middle-class, went to private schools and universities and became lawyers or businessmen. They live in relative luxury and have no real knowledge, hard experience, of the life of the poor of the world, or of the poor even of their own country. And so they make laws that relate badly to the needs of their people.

If you suffer you begin to understand suffering. If you have suffered, it opens the heart; it opens the mind to the experience of most of the people in the world. It gives you the experience which you need to relate correctly to every person.

The reality of the Christ is that He has experienced every human condition, and so He can relate to every human being. You cannot relate to what you have never experienced. That is why it is necessary for people to travel widely and to experience different people, of different colour, tradition, language, mental concepts, to experience the other, that which is not your own habitual experience. In that sense, suffering enables you to be more human than you otherwise would have been.

CONDITIONING

How do we transform the conditioning of daily life into our personal attempt towards the art of living?

By resolving the conflicts which prevent the creation of detachment. We are either attached or free. It is one or the other. Conditioning is slavery, lack of freedom. Freedom is the given state. Conditioning alters that state into one of slavery. We are attached in a state of conflict. Overcome the conflict and suddenly we are in harmony. Then we find there is another conflict. We go deeper. This does not happen in a day.

There is nothing I could tell you to do for the next five minutes that would free you. Nothing that is lasting in the human condition is done like that.

The deep conditioning of oneself is a long process, so you have to work on yourself to be deconditioned. Life itself brings about conditioning. We are human beings and we would not be on planet Earth if that were not the case. If we were on, say, Venus or Mercury, and were eighth-degree initiates, then there would be no question of talking about conditioning.

We condition one another, our children and so on. That is all part of life as we live it. Deconditioning releases you from conditioning and, therefore, attachments. It is a process; you cannot say: "I am going to be detached" from one moment to the next. It is not like that. The more you work on yourself, the more detachment grows.

You sacrifice your need for the attachment. We need the attachment because we need our conditioning. It satisfies us from an astral/emotional point of view. That is why we have to overcome the attachments of the astral plane. First of the physical, then of the astral, then of the mental plane, until we are deconditioned on all three levels. Deconditioned means less and less attached. These are all attachments formed from experiences.

I do not think anybody in the world is polarized on the physical plane any more. The bulk of humanity is polarized on the astral plane. That means it is their seat of consciousness. The attachments formed by their focus on the astral plane through identifying with their emotions (which we take to be real but which are quite unreal, like dreams) condition us. The experiences of the astral plane are unreal. They are nothing more than thoughtforms.

If we attach an emotion onto the thoughtform, we are attached to that. It triggers every time something reminds us of that experience. It triggers the same reaction, and so forms the attachment. Conditioning is another name for attachment.

We do the same thing on the mental plane. It is much more difficult to see on the mental plane because the attachment for most people is emotional. That is called glamour or illusion, but until we see the illusion, become aware of it, we cannot decondition ourselves.

To be attached, to be conditioned, is the same. They are part of the unreality which we call life. But it is unreality which we have to go through because that is how we grow in conscious awareness. If, however, conscious awareness is limited to the astral plane, then we live in that glamour, that illusion, about the nature of life. The nature of life is very different in reality from that sensed by most people because it is sensed as all taking place on the astral plane. Every experience is wrapped up in astral matter, the thoughtforms which tie us to the astral plane. We create the astral plane out of our thoughtforms.

How do we transform the conditioning?

By the discipline of self deconditioning, by the process, the discipline, of becoming more and more detached. That is difficult to do because it needs discipline but in essence is simple. You should practise, therefore, the three rules which Maitreya gives – honesty of mind, sincerity of spirit, and detachment:

Honesty of mind, thinking in a straight line. He says most people think one thing, say something else and do something else again. What we think, what we say and what we do, are all different. There is no honesty of mind.

Sincerity of spirit: we copy one another and condition ourselves by copying. Conditioning is copying by not being yourself. If you are not yourself, then you have to be something else. You have to be something at any given time, and if it is not yourself it is something that is, in part, the not-self. So we are often the not-self.

Occasionally, under certain circumstances, we become sincere in our hearts, in our minds, and act in that way, speak from the heart to the heart. But most people, in much of their actions, relate to other people to impress them, to create a vision in the mind of their companion which is favourable to themselves.

We act a part because we feel that will impress. "They will think highly of me." "They will think I am very intelligent and very sure of myself. Of course, I know I am not sure of myself, but they will think I am if I speak with a loud voice and I come over crisply and strong to them and not so shyly. If I am outgoing and use big gestures they will see I am at home in the world. I can control the world. I know that I cannot control the world. I am scared of the world, but if I give the impression that I am in control of things, they will look up to me, and they will like me. They will make me a friend, and then I will feel happy. I will feel safe. And if I do that with everybody I will have a lot of friends. And if I have a lot of friends, I will be really happy."

That is the insincerity in which many people live. Am I not right? Think of oneself. Is that not the case? How many people are really, utterly and entirely themselves? A child with its parents, yes, because the child as yet is unconditioned. A young child with its parents is absolutely honest until it is corrupted. Then, of course, it acts up and says: "I know if I keep this up I will get what I want. You bet." And so they will cry and cry and cry. Corruption sets in quite early, but at first the child is totally honest. It cries when it is hurt or hungry or tired and it smiles all the rest of the time.

Detachment: how many people are detached? Well, ask yourself how detached do you feel? How free from the need for other people are you? How free from the need for constant praise, the need for constant thanks, are you? So that everything you do, however little it is, they give thanks for, and how you need that thanks. That little bit of praise! It keeps you going. It builds your ego. How can you say you are detached if this is going on all the time?

Look for that which shows you how undetached you are. If someone praises you, does it make any difference to you? Mostly, I think you will find that it does. If you are detached, it should not make any difference whether people are for you or against you, giving praise or unflattering criticism. It should make no difference if you are truly detached. And if you are truly detached, you are not conditioned.

We all suffer from the conditioning that sets in when we are children. Babies are not conditioned, but within a few years conditioning begins. Those of you who have children, think on it, because we make life difficult for our children by conditioning them in what we think is protecting them. It is not on the whole protecting them. It is getting them to do what we want them to do – that is, mainly not be a nuisance.

Honesty of mind, sincerity of spirit, and detachment are the key ways to overcome conditioning.

How should one educate a child in the art of living and Laws of Life without conditioning them?

Do not try. Simple. Leave your child alone. Stop hitting him, for one thing, for everything he does that annoys you. The harm that we do is done from our ignorance of the reality of a child. You do not teach him/her the Laws of Life by saying: "Have you studied Mr Creme's *Laws of Life* today? You did? What did you find?" "I found that they were not his. He got it from one of the Masters!" "Good boy. You can have another biscuit."

A child should not even know or recognize that you were teaching it the Laws of Life. It is up to you to recognize when you condition a child and not try to teach him that Maitreya is in the world and that when he is 12 he can do Transmission Meditation "like mummy and daddy do".

Teach the child, without pressure, to be as harmless as possible, and the way to do that is to be as harmless as possible in relation to the child. The child does what you do. If you are harmless, the child will be harmless. If you are harmful, even though you think you are harmless, then the child will be the same. We pass it on all the time.

What is conditioning, and how can you distinguish it from education in the art of living?

Conditioning is education, but it is wrong, distorted, education. Conditioning is acting, thinking, experiencing the known, that which is not new, that which is already known. And if all your experiences are already known and are actually a function of memory, then they have nothing to do with the art of living. The art of living is essentially new from moment to moment. The essence of the art of living is that every moment is new. It is a creative experience coming from the soul.

We are souls in evolution. Therefore all that pertains in our life which reflects that reality, the soul reality, the creativity of the soul, is in tune with the best art of living. That which is known, that which is already defunct, is simply memory, that which is carried over from the past and is useless but liked, sentimentally held on to, by millions of people, is detrimental to the right structures for the art of living.

The art of living will provide the greatest freedom for the greatest number of people, the greatest opportunities for the greatest number of people, the greatest degree of justice for the greatest number of people. That is the art of living. When, in everything that we do – whether as ordinary individuals or in charge of great enterprises – we create conditions in which the greatest number of people find good, the Common Good is exalted, maintained and strengthened. That is what the art of living is about.

LEISURE, SIMPLICITY AND THE ART OF LIVING

Would you please give us examples contrasting leisure versus time?

Leisure is not doing nothing. Leisure is doing what you would like to do, what rests the body, the mind, the heart, or which allows you the time to do for yourself something over and above what you do for the community. Your time today is usually given to the country in which you live, the community as a whole, for five days in a week. On Saturday and Sunday most people, in a developed country, have free time for leisure. Personally I do not think that is enough. I do not think anyone should be expected to work with full concentration for more than three or three-and-a-half days a week, leaving them four or three-and-a-half days for what I would call leisure.

Leisure might be the most strenuous part of the week. If one is a mountain climber, then it is definitely going to be the hardest thing that one does that week. If one is a long distance runner, again it is going to be tough for three-and-a-half days. If we are engaged in taking a car to pieces and putting it together again, that could be a very hard, concentrated job, but a sheer joy given a certain mentality, with a visual memory for where the parts go back! There are different kinds of leisure and uses of leisure. Time and leisure are not contrasts. One upholds the other.

The goods of the world, to a major extent, are made by the poorest groups in the world, who have no other option but to gather the tea, to make the suits, tools, radios, shoes, etc. The result of that labour is leisure for the people who receive the money when these goods are sold. They live lives of relative luxury and leisure. They can do what they want to do anytime. They can meet with friends and go riding, or go for a trip in the car, or to a cinema. They can take an airplane and go off to Europe or Japan for a few days. Leisure allows you to do all those things you would like to do as if you were on vacation.

It is like having a vacation every week. I think people need space in which to be themselves, find themselves, know and experience themselves. Time-serving, of course, is doing a job.

You cannot contrast leisure and time except to say that those who have time have leisure. If you have the time, you have the leisure. If you do not have the time, you do not have the leisure because you are doing something else. You cannot be happy because you are doing too much that is nothing to do with you. That is a major illness in the world today.

A lot of people are constantly ill. It is a purely emotional and psychological illness because they are spending too much of their time doing what is against their nature and interests. They become mechanical, a machine, and lose touch with their inner selves.

How can we cultivate the attitude of leisure in the midst of our busy lives?

Leisure is not an attitude. Leisure is having the time to do what you want to do, which is bubbling up inside you and you want to do it. Everybody wants to go on vacation. That seems to be bubbling up in everybody all the time. Leisure to me is not going on vacation, not going abroad, not getting on planes, but just going upstairs to my studio, shutting the door, sitting down and looking at what I have been doing. That is leisure, time to be who you are.

Today, when people are at work, mostly they are not who they are. It is a parallel existence. It is their second life or second personality, which they have constructed in order to earn a living and live in this society, corrupt as it is. We have to live in it. We have to be here. Opting out of it will not do us any good. We are in incarnation at this time because of what is happening at this time. We have the task of making a new and better world.

Leisure is doing what you innately want to do, which is to be creative; it is the opportunity to be creative. People forget that creativity is not necessarily about art. There is a question: "If you are not an artist, how do you get a bit of creativity into your life?" It is not necessarily being an artist as a painter, musician, dancer or actor. That is only one branch of activity.

You can be creative in every aspect of life, whatever it is. The major scientists are making extraordinary discoveries about the nature of the atom, for example, about the energetic substance of our universe, how it seems to slip through their fingers, and then suddenly there is no matter any more. What has happened to the matter? Those scientists have made a great discovery. That is creativity, the same creativity as painters who make a picture or musicians a tone poem.

Creativity exists in every single son of God. It is a God-given quality. Creative activity is the nature of life lived under the Laws of Life. The art of living is creative living, which entails all aspects of life. You can be a mechanic, or a nurse, you can be . . . .

How will sharing the world's resources help us to have more leisure time in the developed and developing world?

It will help those in the developing world to have more time because they have to spend so much time creating the little that they have out of nothing. We in the developed world have all the time in the world to create the much that we have out of much. If the world's resources were properly shared according to the needs of the different nations, it would involve only a redistribution of resources. It is all to do with distribution and redistribution. That is the basis of the economic problem today.

Plans for a radical redistribution are already extant. They could be offered to humanity as soon as we accept the principle of sharing. By their very nature, this would give everybody much more leisure time than they have at the moment.

So much of people's time is used up in a purely mechanistic way to fill office blocks, fill up sheets of paper, file them away, take them out, read the files, write stories about them, hand them up to somebody who hands them up to someone else. Somebody signs something. It goes up and down the floors again, simply distributing pieces of paper that report on the various amounts of the different commodities which have been produced or will be produced, and the costs and profits which this will entail. All of that is done over and over again in millions of such office blocks throughout the modern world. It is a complete waste of human talent, energy and imagination. It makes terrible inroads into the possible leisure that people could have.

These are not real jobs. They are completely constructed jobs to do with globalization and making sure that T-shirts made in Japan, China, Hong Kong or Costa Rica, and sold in the American market, are of such and such a design and quality. It is still to do with the distribution of resources. Most of our trade is recorded in this way.

The most numerous relics we have of the Egyptian civilization are the reports on their trade. The cuneiform records, these massive amounts of tablets, are to do with: "Sold today three fish, one waste paper basket, two melons to so and so, received eight pesetas," or whatever the coin was. They are solid, baked clay and took up a huge amount of space. What good does it do us to know this? It gives us a little view of the daily running of an Egyptian state thousands of years ago.

If someone really insane wants to see how the people of the 20th and 21st centuries lived, they only have to look in the files of any of these huge skyscrapers, go through them for hundreds of years; devote their time and energy to reading the printing on these files, and then reading the emails to do with these files. They will get a very clear picture of the life of the nonentities who wrote them.

What purpose would that serve? An enormous amount of time and energy of fellow human beings is wasted today by those who run the mechanics of the world, the production and sale of the multifarious and useless objects which are duplicated until there is no end to them. All to give us multiple choice. How many different ice-creams do we need? Is 50 enough? There are shops that sell more than the proverbial 50.

The same goes for every kind of commodity that we produce today in every developed country.

Almost nothing that America, Britain, France, Japan or anywhere else produce is needed by any other country. The objects are all produced to give 'choice' or the latest gadget to fit to the other gadgets which we already have and produce.

It is a useless waste of human potential. When we share the resources of the world, we will get rid of a great deal of that. We need only keep records of the goods that have been exchanged by using the sophisticated form of barter which sharing will bring about. It will be totally simplified; our life will be simplified out of all recognition. We are not going to have even 50 different kinds of ice-cream. I know it is hard!

Could you elaborate on what role simplicity has in the art of living from your talk?

Simplicity has a role to play because as the path of evolution is followed, you find that all creatures, first of all, want to do nothing but eat. Then as the organisms become more and more complex, so their needs become more complex. Then you get human beings, a massive 6.5 billion of us on planet Earth, living the most complicated lives, creating an infinite number of goods of all kinds, usable and unusable, useful and useless, which are filling the shops and the storehouses of the whole world. That is not to count the millions of tons of useless armaments which clutter and threaten the world.

Just take a walk down one of the main avenues in Tokyo, for example, and go to the area where you can buy technology of all kinds; mobile phones, cameras, televisions or computers. You can buy millions of them. Every building is filled, absolutely, from the first floor to the 20th, with nothing but all kinds of communication gadgets.

Will it get simpler? Is simplicity a part of it? I would say that simplicity is very much to do with the art of living. My experience is that as humanity grows and life becomes more and more filled with objects, with technologies, it becomes less and less simple, and it goes further away from what we are calling the art of living. We do not know how to live. It is not a good way to live, to fill storehouses with all those cell phones and computers. They should be distributed if useful, or not made if useless. It is commercialization gone mad.

As we evolve, as the art of living develops in humanity, as we are willing to give up somewhat this complicated overproduction, we will find that simplicity is the keynote.

Simplicity is really using the minimum that you need to enjoy the fullest life. The fullest life can be lived as an art, but it needs simplicity. So that when we enter the New Age properly; when the art of living is taken seriously by humanity and is being recognized and developed; when harmlessness and the Law of Sacrifice are controlling it, then you will find a greater and greater simplicity also. The 'wilderness experience' will show humanity the need for simplicity. And the more complex the life, as in, perhaps, America today, the more difficult it may be to accept the simplicity of the future. But it will be a happier time because there is great happiness to be had in simplicity.

NATURE OF INTUITION

Since intuition is so key to the art of living our lives, can you shed more light on how we can tap into our intuition or recognize an intuitive thought, given our point in evolution, which is not even mentally polarized for most of us?

Intuition is the function of the soul. The only way you can tap into your intuition is to use it. You may not know when you are doing it or when you are not doing it. You may confuse your intuition, as people do, with astral imagination. Very often people think that that is intuition because it is not their everyday thought, but it may be purely astral. If it is not astral, it may come from a higher level, the soul. It can only come from the soul if sufficient contact is made with the soul.

The intuition is actually not developed so much as invoked. Read the Master DK, the Alice Bailey Teachings, for example. We may understand the words but not what they mean. We understand that this is abstract thought, it is esotericism, and therefore it is difficult. It is meant to be difficult. If it were easy we would understand it with our brain.

The intuition comes into play when we invoke it to help understand that which was written above the level of the lower mind. That is a Master's work. We may get a sense of the meaning of what He is writing, but we could not put it into our own words, we have not understood it enough to do that.

But by reading it again and again, and then putting it aside and coming back to it, we get to understand more and more because we are really invoking the intuition. Our soul, through the intuition, at the manasic level, is investing us with its insights. We are stretching our mind until it is encompassing the higher mental planes, and the intuition comes into play. That we can do. That is a definite way in which we can expand the intuition. I do not know any other way in which we can, except by meditating more.

I have been conscious all my working life as a painter that I had been meditating even long before I actually took up meditation. Every picture I painted, I felt afterwards, was a state of meditation. All the time I would be searching for the right tone of a colour or the exact angle of a form. Without thinking of anything else except that, just the problems of painting, I would be invoking the intuition. There are no other answers to it.

That picture had never been before. I was making it for the first time, so the problems were there for the first time. Every time I painted, and this is still the same, it is as if I am starting painting for the first time. A new picture is like my first picture. I am on tenterhooks. I really do not know how it will be. You have to get into the deep concentration that invokes the intuition.

These purely pictorial decisions are creative acts. It is a big phrase, "creative act". It need not be a great masterpiece. It is simply that the process of doing it is invoking the intuition. Likewise, when you read something like the Master DK's teachings (I do not mean novels and so on), you invoke the intuition. Try reading *The Laws of Life,* the thoughts and ideas of Maitreya, without invoking the intuition. I doubt if you would understand very much.

Intuition is certainly something that can be invoked and expanded. Like everything, the more you do it, the more you can do it, until it is automatic. You bring in the light of the soul. You do not sit down and visualize a beam of light coming down onto the problem, but you lift your attention to a level where your soul can, through the intuition, enlighten you, give you the answer.

". . . or recognize an intuitive thought . . ." When it is intuitive, you can recognize it. It is when it is not intuitive that you might be confused. When it is astral, astral imagination, you might think: "It was not me. It was my intuition." But was it? Find out where it came from. *". . . given our point in evolution, which is not even mentally polarized for most of us."*

If you are under 1.5 and not yet mentally polarized, therefore, you must take into account that sometimes it will be astral glamour rather than the intuition that is guiding your activity. But that is not to say that it is not the intuition. The soul can be contacted by anybody coming up to the first initiation. It is the soul which brings people to the first initiation. You take the first initiation at a certain time but you might have been a whole lifetime in coming to that state from 0.9 or 0.8. It is a process. It takes time to come about. Evolution proceeds slowly. Since it does, it lasts; evolution sticks.

How would I know whether my good, positive hunches or inspirations are intuition or just astral? Are there techniques we might be ready to use for developing intuition?

I spoke about reading the Master DK, expanding the range of the mind. When we expand the mind we approach the intuition, the levels where lower mind can no longer take us. If we do this all the time, it develops.

CREATIVITY AND ART

I am not aware of any artistic talent. How can I better integrate creativity into my daily life?

As I said, it is not a question of artistic talent. It is a question of creative action in any department of life. It is creativity, not artistic talent, we are talking about.

If someone is an artist, is it better to create art and follow their passion than to take a regular job to support the Reappearance work?

It is better to support the Reappearance work but that can be done in any kind of work, including art.

Is being an artist a service to humanity even if you are not a Rembrandt?

That depends on how far from being a Rembrandt you are. If you are talking about making little seaside pictures to remind people of their vacations and selling them in the shops dedicated to that activity, then I do not think it is a great service to humanity. But people find art at their own level. Pictures decorate the wall. They may remind people of a nice holiday, but that is not art, it is only a picture. The English have a phrase: "Every picture tells a story." If it tells a story, it is a good picture. If it does not tell a story, it is a bad picture. That is how many people look at art. Art has nothing to do with either storytelling or holidays. Art is a function totally of its own. It is a language for speaking about the nature of reality. You do that at a very high level if you are a Rembrandt, and at a very low level if you are Joe Bloggs.

If so, can you say something about the process of providing this service and what makes it so? For instance, does it have to do simply with the act of creating or is it more to do with the product of the creation?

It is more to do with the act of creating rather than the product. There may be no end product of the creativity. There may be a great scientific discovery or a great discovery in the learning process, a teaching process, or some religious revelation or new philosophical truth. In talking about the art of living, living is an art form as it responds to the Laws of Life and creates harmony, synthesis, beauty and unity.

THE REAPPEARANCE WORK AND TRANSMISSION MEDITATION

How much should we emphasize in our Reappearance work educating the public about rebirth, harmlessness, karma and sacrifice?

These are the laws underlying the art of living. It is an art and needs certain guidelines. These are the guidelines, the starting points, for the art of living must obey these laws. They are fundamental for right human relationships. Without harmlessness there cannot be right relationship. Without rebirth there can be no life. You cannot do anything about a law like the Law of Karma and the Law of Rebirth. You must simply recognize them. You can expand on or present these laws to a greater or lesser degree. It is up to yourself.

How much control can we exert over ourselves at this stage?

What you have control over is your degree of harmlessness or otherwise, your capacity for sacrifice or otherwise. These are the only things that you can control. The others are major laws that govern life itself on planet Earth, so you have to work within them. That is how you can present the idea of harmlessness and the associated fact of rebirth as fundamentals to our life on planet Earth.

They are not something you have to acquire. They already exist. What does not exist is harmlessness in all people all of the time.

One of the things that struck me while you were talking was that great artists recreate old masterpieces. I started thinking how you take the Alice Bailey teachings, a quote from the Bible, your Master's articles, and totally recreate them, not just copy them, when you give your talks. I have been thinking since yesterday about how most of the time when I talk to people about the Reappearance I am merely copying. How can I recreate what I have learned and speak from the heart and make what I say uniquely my own?

If you have been talking about the Reappearance for as many years as I have (about 35 years) you have to make it your own or bust! Can you imagine what it would be like for the audience if every time you spoke you reiterated, word for word, Alice Bailey or what you yourself said in the first years of your talks? It is something that develops. If you are involved in it (and you would not do it for long if you were not really involved in it), you do make it your own. You cannot help it. It is a process of re-creation. You use the necessary elements of the story that could go on for hours, but in a talk you have to bring it all down and speak from the heart. It has to be in your heart to begin with. You can only speak from the heart when it is in your heart.

As I go on to the stage I have no idea what I am going to say. I know the ideas which must come into the talk. I have no idea where they will come in, how many will come in, what I will forget, what I will leave out. In San Francisco, this year, I said this talk could be given from many different points of view. I could not think of mine! Then I just said: "What are you going to do about your President? What are you going to do about your government?" The audience laughed. Immediately, our rapport was established. Then they listened to what was being said, and I just spoke. When I speak, I just speak. I have no a priori idea of what I am going to say.

I just speak as it comes. I say a word and that links up to another word, which makes me think of another idea and I bring that in. Then I say a word, and that brings in another word and that idea has to come in. It is part of the information. I am giving information, but hopefully not dry information. I am trying to make it an interesting discourse on a lot of subjects, and bring the whole thing together until the audience has a view of the world, the state of the world, and what is needed. You just bring everything you have into it. It is therefore a living process. I cannot repeat it. I have never exactly repeated a lecture. I immediately forget what I have said.

How does Transmission Meditation play a part in enhancing or helping the art of living?

Inevitably it does. It helps you to get on with life, feel better, happier, more sound, more in equilibrium. Like all meditations Transmission Meditation brings you into closer contact with the soul. It does it more perfectly than most because it is 100 per cent scientific. Transmission Meditation enhances the quality of your soul contact. Doing Transmission Meditation brings you into contact with all the inspiring thoughts and ideas that surround it, like the Reappearance of the Christ and the Masters. It keeps foremost in your mind the idea of service because it is a service to the world. It is a never-ending reservoir of energy which the group can use as needed from the store of energy which they are creating all the time.

You cannot do Transmission Meditation without evolving quickly. You cannot but evolve with the energies pouring through the chakras in an enhanced state. You cannot evolve so quickly by any other means. So it is very much a method of enhancing the quality of your art of living.

How best can we do Transmission Meditation? By doing it more correctly, keeping aligned. It is all to do with alignment.

PART TWO

THE PAIRS OF OPPOSITES

THE PAIRS OF OPPOSITES
by the Master –, through Benjamin Creme

Since man first emerged on Earth, his history has been one of conflict and strife, aggression and war. Seldom has there been a time when these tendencies have not been uppermost, until it would seem that they represent the essential nature of man. Yet, despite all evidence to the contrary, this is emphatically not the case. Why, then, does man present such a distorted image of himself? From whence comes this capacity for chaotic action and destructive violence?

Man is essentially a soul, a perfect reflection of God. Through countless incarnations over untold ages, man's soul seeks to express its divine nature in time and space. Creating for itself a physical counterpart, the soul endows that with the means of evolution to its own perfection. Thus does the Plan of God work out.

The key to this development is aspiration. Indwelling in all men is the desire for perfection and the urge to express the good, the beautiful and the true – the attributes of the soul. No one, however faltering in action, is bereft of this desire for betterment, however expressed. In no one does this longing not exist.

How then to account for man's aberrations, his violence and hate?

The answer lies in man's unique position, the meeting ground of spirit and matter, and the tensions which their

73

concurrence evokes. Man is an immortal soul, plunged in matter, subject, therefore, to the limitations which that matter imposes. His struggle for perfection involves the bringing into total union and resolution of these twin poles of his nature. Through repeated incarnations, the evolutionary process gradually achieves this aim, until the quality and radiation of the matter coincides with that of spirit. The Plan is fulfilled and another Son of God has returned home.

For long ages, the dominance of matter precludes a major expression of the soul; evolution proceeds but slowly. When, at long last, the opposing poles of his nature are resolved, man realizes that the dichotomy is but seeming, the oppositions unreal. Then he sees that all is One, spirit and matter but two aspects of one divine Whole, the limitations of the past naught but illusion.

Without the struggle of opposites and the friction which ensues, man's progress would be slow indeed. Friction is the fire which impels him on his way, aspiration the light which calls him ever upwards. Thus does man discard, in time, the limitations of matter, endowing it with the radiance of his spiritual truth. Man's task is to spiritualize matter and to bring the substance of the planet, in every kingdom, into a perfect reflection of the Heavenly Man Whose body it is. Conflict and war, violence and hate, are but the passing manifestation of man's inability, as yet, to demonstrate his true nature. The time is fast coming when his truth will prevail, his beauty radiate and his good demonstrate for all to see. (*Share International*, July 1989)

COMMENTARY ON THE PAIRS OF OPPOSITES

This chapter is based on an edited version of a talk given by Benjamin Creme at the Transmission Meditation Conference held near San Francisco, USA, in August 2002. (First published in **Share International** *magazine, January/February 2003.)*

'The Pairs of Opposites' is probably the most important subject that one could think about – nothing less than the demonstration by my Master of the fundamental fact of our existence as souls; and why it is difficult for the soul, and also difficult for us, humanity, to do much as a soul for a very long time. Of course, from the point of view of the soul it is no time at all, because the soul does not function in time. But from the point of view of that through which it functions – the physical bodies, in succession, over all the ages – it is a seemingly endless period of time before the soul can actually demonstrate its nature through its reflection, the man or woman in incarnation. Of course, it does not happen all at once. The soul incarnates in matter. It provides itself with bodies – physical, emotional and mental – synthesized by the personality, the reflection of the soul on the physical plane. The difference in vibration between the soul and the bodies precludes any instant, or even early, fusion of the two.

Man first emerged on Earth 18.5 million years ago, according to the Masters. That is a long time. We have been at it for all that time. Can you imagine how tiring that would be if you remembered it? Eighteen-and-a-half million years seems an inordinately long time for humanity to have struggled to this point.

Well, it seems that there has seldom been a time when we were not having conflict and strife, aggression and war. Who said that this country, America, was discovered by Columbus? No, the Vikings came long before that. In the 8th century they landed here, painted themselves, and then they found and fought other people who were painted even more so.

"Seldom has there been a time when these tendencies have not been uppermost." Can you imagine, over 18.5 million years there was seldom a quiet weekend. There was always some war just starting, or they were resting, waiting for Monday to start again, until it would seem that this represents our essential nature. Is this true? Is it possible that this is the intrinsic nature of man, humanity?

The Master says that despite all evidence to the contrary (and of course, there is massive evidence to the contrary) this is emphatically not the case. If a Master says that, He knows. The Masters know because They see a time and a state in which this is not the case. The essential nature of man and, of course, woman, is other than conflict, strife, aggression and war. Why then do we present such a terrible image, a totally distorted image, of our real nature?

"Whence comes this capacity for chaotic action and destructive violence?" Every generation, according to the esoteric teaching, brings into incarnation those equipped with the ability to solve the problems of the time. This ensures that the evolution of humanity goes on; that there is always a new generation which sees the problems and can deal with them in a new way; can resolve them and prepare the way forward for the rest of humanity. At the same time, of course, there is this tendency, inherent in the relationship of spirit to matter, which produces conflict.

"Man is essentially a soul, a perfect reflection of God." This is the esoteric truism of all time. We are really souls in incarnation – perfect souls identical with what we call God, the

Heavenly Man Who ensouls this planet, Who has created us, for Whom we are thoughtforms in His mind. He has envisioned a plan of evolution and fitted us into it as one aspect of the Plan, by no means the whole of it, but one important aspect: bringing spirit and matter together in man.

"Through countless incarnations, over untold ages. . ." Eighteen-and-a-half million years! When did our souls begin to take heed of the matter through which they were expressing themselves on the physical plane? That determines our point in evolution. The moment our soul sees that we are ready to begin to express, somewhat, its perfection; to bring the qualities of the soul – truth, beauty, intelligence, the longing for perfection itself – into the incarnational process, the true evolution of the man or woman begins. The time when that happened in each individual case determines our point in evolution.

Through countless incarnations, the soul seeks to express its divine nature in time and space through successive personalities: through bodies, physical, emotional and mental, sometimes as a man, sometimes as a woman. It carries out this desire, this longing to replicate its nature and quality, in a physical counterpart. The soul endows its reflection with the means of evolution to its own perfection. In this way, the Plan of God works out.

Millions of people do not know that there is a Plan. That is an unfortunate state of affairs. I think it is probably the most unfortunate, second to the almost total ignorance that we are souls. The first thing, the first reality, it seems to me, that everyone should be taught is the human constitution: that we are essentially spiritual in nature, and that that divinity or spirit reflects itself at a somewhat lower vibration as the human soul, and that the soul reflects itself on the physical plane as a man or woman. Evolution takes place according to a Plan. The Masters of our Spiritual Hierarchy are the Custodians of this Plan.

If everyone in the world knew that, or could even take it as a hypothesis, the world would be extraordinarily different. Because people do not know that there is a Plan, they have no idea where they are heading. They are driven along by the great magnet of evolution, and the result is they have really no free will. They are simply driven by circumstance, and they react to the circumstance, of course, from the point of evolution that they have reached.

What is needed, I would say probably above everything else, is a re-education of humanity so that we know that evolution proceeds according to a Plan, and that we can take part in that Plan. We can become conscious and work according to the Plan. The chaos, aggression and war, the conflict and strife, are the result of ignorance of the fact of the Plan and its nature. Therefore, we do not know how to live. There are great laws governing this process of evolution, and the soul provides its vehicle with the means to evolve.

Aspiration

The key to this development is called aspiration. Everything that evolves, from a grain of sand up to the most evolved Being you could imagine, the most exalted angel or Avatar you could visualize, has reached that point as a result of aspiration.

There was a time when life lived in the sea. The seas carried the vast majority of the life of this planet. On the land areas there were the beginnings of the vegetable kingdom, and some sea creatures came out of the sea onto land.

It must have been an extraordinary experience for the first fish or reptiles that came out of the sea onto the relatively drier land. They had to learn to breathe and start moving in a different way. They had to learn to walk, clumsily at first, and then with great facility until they could run faster than a horse runs today.

This did not happen by chance but as a result of aspiration. It is difficult to imagine the aspiration of a sea creature to go onto the land, and yet without aspiration it would never have happened. No change takes place without the aspiration for change. A change of that nature, from living in the sea to living on the land, is momentous. It was obeying an inner will, an aspiration for change, for betterment, for a higher state, for a perfection as yet undreamed of but felt as a possibility. We evolve in exactly the same way.

Through aspiration we have our idealism. We react to the energies which are sent into the world by the Hierarchy of Masters, the Custodians of the Plan, and in response we aspire to change. We have a vision of a different and better, a more perfect, state – whether that is political, economic, social, or scientific, cultural or whatever. We evolve through this capacity to envisage something better, something closer to the perfection that we instinctively know is possible. We instinctively know what is in the mind of the Logos because we are fundamentally souls, exact reflections of the Logos Whom we call God, the Logos of planet Earth, the Heavenly Man Whose idea we are.

In this way we evolve, create new conditions. We can jump out of the sea and get used to living on dry land.

"The key to this development is aspiration. Indwelling in all men is the desire for perfection and the urge to express the good, the beautiful and the true – the attributes of the soul. No one, however faltering in action, is bereft of this desire for betterment, however expressed." Maybe there are some exceptions. There are some modern politicians, and some politicians of the past, whom it is difficult to place in that context. But let us be generous. Let us accept what the Master says: that no one – however faltering in action, inadequate, grasping for power, greedy – is bereft of the desire for

betterment. He senses the good. He misinterprets it of course, totally, and creates mayhem.

"How then to account for man's aberrations, his violence and hate?" How can you account for some of the men who rule the world at this time?

Meeting of Spirit and Matter

"The answer lies in man's unique position, the meeting ground of spirit and matter, and the tensions which their concurrence evokes." That is the secret of it all. We are souls – perfect, sublime, spiritual beings, identical with the God from Which we come. But we are wrapped up in the opposite, or what is apparently the opposite: the matter of our physical, emotional and mental bodies. Even our mental body, even that tenuous thing called thought, is matter, expressing itself on a particular level. In that matter a great reorganization takes place. We call it evolution. The soul incarnates in matter and goes through the long, seemingly endless conflict between that which we call spirit and what we call matter.

That is the reason for the endless violence and hatred through the ages – 18.5 million years – until at times humanity was almost exterminated. Much of the killing was done by the animal kingdom, but much of it was done by man to man, for food, for land, for greedy dominance of his territory. Man has a greedy side, stemming from his misunderstanding of the meaning and purpose of life. Some men think it is all right to grab another person's land, to set up shop there and call it 'the Empire'.

Imperialism is nearly as old as humanity, and it is still going on. There is still this urge for the bigger and better. Of course, the bigger and the better we are, the more powerful we are, so we can become even bigger and better. This is what all imperialistic countries have done throughout time. It is the way the Romans conquered all the known world, the whole of Europe and Asia Minor, all the way to India and in the West to Germany and the lowlands, France, Spain and even across the channel to Britain.

Look at what the Romans did. They were everywhere, but they were not satisfied with that. So what did they do? When the world was opened up by other peoples, the Spaniards and Portuguese and so on, who sent their discoverers all over the world, the Romans awoke again and said: "This is no good at all. We have lost our power. Nobody thinks of Rome any more." And so the Romans reincarnated as the English. They set about conquering the world again, and this time they got most of it, about three-quarters, which they called the British Empire. That is imperialism for you.

Reincarnating as the English made it possible to build a bigger empire than Rome had ever known. The Romans built roads; the English built railroads. They could go further and faster, and it has opened up the world. The Romans are still at it.

"Man is an immortal soul plunged in matter, subject, therefore, to the limitations which that matter imposes." That is the problem. It is all to do with the level of vibration. Matter, relatively speaking, in relation to the soul, is inert. It does not vibrate, or it vibrates so slowly that for long ages the soul cannot use it except in a very rudimentary way, in that it incarnates, and produces a vehicle, a man or woman, who grows up and has children and dies. We have all done that. This is the way it progresses, but it takes forever.

Matter is inert, non-responsive to the vibration of the soul, to what the Master calls the beauty, the truth, the good, of the soul. And yet the Being in this body, locked into matter, has – because he or she is a soul – a longing for perfection, the sense that there is something better. There comes a time in everyone's incarnational history when the soul looks down at its reflection and says: "Look, look at this." It brings its friends. "Look, look! You see? He is moving. Look. He moved again. Did you see that? You must have seen it. Look, look! There, he moved again. He did."

That reminds me of a time on the ship the Queen Mary where we had a number of Transmission Meditations. On one occasion, we were inside at deck level, in a beautiful round room doing Transmission Meditation. It was a weekend and the public were allowed on the boat which was now a floating hotel, at Long Beach, California. We were all sitting there near the round portholes, and the crowds were going round. We could hear them, but we were meditating happily, when suddenly there was a family just behind me, who in a loud voice said: "Oh, look at these. These are dummies. Look, look! You know, it is like those waxworks at Madame Tussaud's. These are waxworks. Look at them all sitting." We could hardly restrain our laughter. And then there was: "They are not dummies! Look. One moved. That one moved." "Where? I didn't see him move." "Yes. There he goes again." We got stiffer, trying not to laugh. They went away eventually, unsure of what they had seen.

So it is for the soul when it looks down, and it sees a little spiritual effort in its counterpart. A little light is shown emanating from this inert matter and the soul brings its counterpart, its vehicle, into meditation of some kind. Through meditation, the soul eventually brings matter to be more responsive to its nature.

There was then introduced a means of linking or fusing the soul and its counterpart, by which means the man or woman could respond to the soul's impact. It is called initiation. The initiations, five in number, were brought in to take advantage of the point reached by the advanced humanity of the time, and through that process the link with the soul deepened. The fusing process developed, and the evolution of humanity progressed.

This is an artificial process which speeds up the evolutionary process. But for initiation, it would take millions more years of tension, struggling, aggression and war to bring about that fusing, yoga, that union of spirit and matter. Once a person has come to the beginning of the initiatory experience – which covers the last few lives only of the long evolution – the whole process speeds up.

"His struggle for perfection involves the bringing into total union and resolution of these twin poles of his nature." That is the necessity, to bring into total union two extreme opposites, as they appear to be: the resplendent, beautiful, good and true spiritual nature of the soul, and the inertia, the low vibration, of matter.

"Through repeated incarnations the evolutionary process gradually achieves this aim, until the quality and the radiation of the matter coincides with that of spirit. The Plan is fulfilled and another Son of God has returned home." When it is fully achieved, the fifth of the five initiations is taken and the Master stands free from the pull of matter. There is a total fusion between the soul and its reflection, between that of which the soul is the reflection – the spirit, the monad of the Being – and the physical-plane counterpart, the man or woman you see when you look in the mirror. When these two are fused together the journey on Earth is over. It is only a stepping-stone to another great expansion of consciousness, on cosmic levels, but as far as this planet is concerned the task is done.

"For long ages the dominance of matter precludes a major expression of the soul; evolution proceeds but slowly. When at long last the opposing poles of his nature are resolved man realizes that the dichotomy is but seeming, the oppositions unreal." What brings these opposing poles of his nature into resolution? That is the secret of the evolutionary process. The

ray which controls the human evolution above all others is the 4th ray of Harmony through Conflict. Essentially the aim of man, the inner urge of all people, is to create harmony, unity. Everyone, according to the Master, has inborn the longing for unity, harmony, perfection, reflecting the good, the beautiful and the true, the nature of the soul.

4th ray of Harmony

The way in which this is magically performed by means of the 4th ray is by providing the vitalizing force, the friction which drives a man or woman along the evolutionary path. That is the human condition. All aggression, violence and hatred are points of tension and conflict with which we grapple. Together, these constitute the friction which results from being subject to the 4th ray of Harmony through Conflict. In the end it does produce harmony. The aim of all people governed by the 4th ray is to produce harmony, whether they realize it or not, or whether they can do it or not. Fourth-ray people are often full of conflict because they exemplify this struggle which drives all humanity forward. If there is no conflict there is no movement.

Of course, if we could immediately manifest on the physical plane the harmony – the love, intelligence, will-to-good, the beauty, the truth – of the soul, there would be no need for conflict, but unfortunately we cannot because of the difference in level of vibration. The matter of our physical, astral and mental bodies is inadequate for long ages to express the vibrational rate, and therefore the nature, of the soul. So we do not see the good, the beautiful, the true, which are the soul's nature. They cannot be given expression.

We have an instrument which we must bring more and more into line, and this struggle produces the fire which makes it possible. That, together with the sense of perfection, the aspiration, drives us forward and upward to something we do not yet see; something we sense to be there, something higher and more perfect, like dry land for a sea creature. Can you imagine what that step was? It is the same step of a benighted individual on the physical plane who does not yet know the nature of the soul, or see him or herself as a soul, to picture what it is like to see as the soul sees. It is the same step in consciousness.

"Without the struggle of opposites and the friction which ensues, man's progress would be slow indeed." The 4th ray of Harmony through Conflict is driving humanity forward. It is that ray which deals with the pairs of opposites. The way in which the 4th ray does this, when handled correctly, is to find the path between the pairs of opposites. That, for the 4th-ray person, is the ideal way of bringing these two aspects of our existence into resolution. This of course is very difficult to do and is why it takes a long time. But the 4th ray is the most powerful ray for humanity in this respect. There are other rays – like the 5th ray which is dominating the mental evolution – but the 4th ray is precisely the ray that helps us to resolve the pairs of opposites. It is done by having not too great a care for either.

The 4th-ray type, in dealing with the pairs of opposites, ideally does not identify with either spirit or matter. It is this which gives to the 4th ray of a lower nature an appearance of being amoral, of not being involved in moral certitudes. It is a mutable, uncommitted state in which the 4th-ray type does not identify with matter and does not identify too much with spirit either. If we do not identify too much with spirit or too much with matter, we can walk that narrow space between the two. That is the perfect way for the development of the 4th-ray individual.

Something like this pertains for all humanity because all humanity, of whatever ray, is governed in its evolutionary sense by this 4th ray of Harmony through Conflict. The conflict in the beginning is needed to create the fire which drives us forward. Without the conflict there would be no movement. But there comes a time when the developed type of all rays has to resolve these two aspects of our nature. We are all souls, and we are all involved in matter. How to resolve it? To resolve it, I suggest to you, is to take the way of the 4th ray and to walk between the pairs of opposites, which means not identifying too much with either. It means not being fanatical. It means, in a word, being detached.

Detachment

This is the essence of detachment, and it is only through detachment that you can make that journey between the pairs of opposites. That is why Maitreya puts detachment at the very core of His teaching. Not only Maitreya; all teaching of a spiritual nature posits detachment as the great method of overcoming this duality of our nature – being both souls, spirit, and matter at one and the same time – and so overcoming conflict and creating harmony by freeing ourselves from identifying with our physical body, our emotions or the constructions of our mind, as the Self. Thus, in that detached state, making a simple journey between these two opposing aspects of our nature.

Detachment is the key and aspiration the driving force. The conflict has been the fire which drives us forward, but the aspiration is that which lifts us higher. Even a Master is aspiring. What the aspiration of a Master is, I cannot tell you, but even a Master aspires to something higher. Even what we call the God of our solar system aspires to a higher form of solar system. The God, the Heavenly Man ensouling a planet, aspires to the idea of creating on His planet a perfect world according to His own ideas of perfection. It is a creative process. As we control the physical, emotional and the mental elementals which constitute the matter of these bodies, so we gradually gain control over this evolutionary process.

The key is radiation. When we come to a certain point we create a radiatory activity in the matter. That comes, of course, from the soul. It fulfils its function on the physical plane through the physical, astral and mental bodies, and they all begin to radiate. It is the soul spiritualizing matter. In each incarnation from then on we bring into our bodies more and more matter of a subatomic nature. They change gradually from atomic to subatomic, which is literally light. We respond more and more to the light of the soul until this becomes dominant in our life as an individual. We no longer identify with the matter, but we are in control of its nature. Through the soul, the bodies are endowed with the radiatory quality which the initiate brings to bear in each life until, through the five initiations, perfection is achieved: the matter of the body of the 5th-degree Master is totally light. It has arrived at perfection as far as this planet is concerned. God in a deeper sense is known, but also through aspiration the Master receives a hint, a glimpse of the way ahead, of what is called The Way of the Higher Evolution, about which we can know almost nothing. Through His aspiration the Master gets a glimpse of that far-flung kingdom, or experience, or condition, in which He can function more luminously, more potently and more creatively than He could at any time, even as a Master, on this planet.

This atomic transformation proceeds first of all through our physical bodies, then through our work with the animal, vegetable and mineral kingdoms. The substance of the planet in every kingdom becomes, in the end, a perfect reflection of the Heavenly Man, the Logos of our planet, Whose body it is.

"Conflict and war, violence and hate, are but the passing manifestations of man's inability, as yet, to demonstrate his true nature." Man's true nature is an immortal soul, a perfect

expression of the Logos of our planet Whose qualities are goodness, beauty and truth. When all of that is achieved throughout the planet, when all kingdoms in nature are perfected, spiritualized in this way, the Heavenly Man's work is over, and He goes on to higher work on a higher planet. We go on to higher work on higher planets, on higher solar systems occasionally, and so it goes on endlessly, on and on, into infinity.

THE PAIRS OF OPPOSITES

QUESTIONS AND ANSWERS

Edited version of the Question and Answer session with Benjamin Creme from the 2002 Transmission Meditation Conferences held in San Francisco, USA, and Kerkrade, the Netherlands.

SERVICE AND CO-OPERATION

How does service help in resolving the pairs of opposites?

Service is one of the two main levers of evolution: one is meditation, the other is service. Service, of whatever kind, gradually distances you from yourself. As your service grows, expands outwards from yourself, you do not lose touch with yourself but you become less and less concerned with your own ego, your personality expression. Service is the impulse of the soul, the carrying out of soul purpose. The soul incarnates to serve the Plan of evolution, which is to spiritualize matter. Incarnating again and again, the soul creates a series of vehicles which gradually become more adept at carrying out the soul purpose and increasing the range of contacts for the soul on the physical plane. These contacts are points of service to the community, the nation, to humanity at large. The higher the state of evolution, usually the more expansive is the range of service. Whether it is a narrow or a wide range, it allows the soul to radiate its Beingness in service to the world.

The soul seeks to serve; it inspires its vehicle, the personality, to serve in particular ways and means. As that happens we become less and less interested in the personality aspect and more and more concerned in altruistic service for the benefit of all. The soul always seeks altruistic action and service. It is not concerned with itself and has no sense of being an individual, separate self. The soul knows nothing of separation. It sees only the whole, and itself in relation to the whole. When the personality is responding correctly to the impulse of the soul it seeks to distance the personality from not only the results of the service but of the service itself. The act of service then becomes a soul-initiated process which means that the person is working with detachment, without glamour.

It is all about detachment. Whatever aids detachment aids us in resolving the pairs of opposites. Nothing so helps detachment as service done in a completely detached way. Then the soul makes real progress on the physical plane through its vehicle. The aspiration of the soul is high, driving the person upward. The fire of action, the creation of an engine which drives us forward, is the conflict which, while we are living in a physical body, we cannot avoid. The conflict continues until we resolve the pairs of opposites. Then we find that that which drove us forward is no longer needed. That is not only a help in resolving the pairs of opposites, it is the way, *par excellence*, of resolving them.

Is co-operation and consensus the way to come to terms with the pairs of opposites in group work?

These are all very much related questions. Co-operation is a result of soul impulse. The soul always seeks harmony and in order to create that harmony consensus becomes necessary. Consensus, when it functions correctly, is really the ability of a group of people to think and act alike, not by reducing their different thoughts and ideas to one single idea held by the strongest person in the group; rather it comes when all the different ideas and points of view of the group are held in space, so to speak, and, intuitively, the souls of the individuals in the group come to a realization that such and such is the way to go. It is always reached as a result of soul experience.

Co-operation is a group intention; the soul co-operates with the Plan of evolution, it comes into incarnation to further that Plan. It lowers itself and spends endless aeons shackled in a physical body through which it cannot express its Being until, nearing the very end of that process, it finally manages to invest its vehicle with enough of its qualities, of its higher vibration, therefore, to enable the personality to express somewhat more of the intention of the soul.

Has the struggle between the pairs of opposites inside the Emergence groups been beneficial or destructive in its purpose?

When we resolve to any degree the pairs of opposites, then to that degree it is beneficial. To the degree that this has not been the case, of course, it may be destructive.

Every group without exception has phases when one or other of these conditions would apply. We cannot say that a group is always destructive because its members never resolve the pairs of opposites, or is always constructive because they always resolve the pairs of opposites. This is not, I think, a real question. The struggle between the pairs of opposites is endemic, it is in the world; it is because we are here that the struggle exists, because we are souls immersed in matter.

In groups of this kind, you can be sure that the beneficial aspects of this struggle are yours, because whatever you do, however you struggle, in a cause of this kind; however you work, totally efficiently or moderately efficiently, totally along the right lines or moderately along the right lines, you are working for the most important event, the most important cause in this world for the last 98,000 years. Nothing that you do, whatever the struggle in doing it, could be more beneficial than this work. Now is the opportunity, as Maitreya put it, of a thousand lifetimes. Never in a thousand lifetimes will you be given this opportunity again. It is something that is difficult to get across, it takes a vision, an understanding of all that is involved, to see the importance and to bring from yourself a response, aliveness, spirit, fire, to do the work and keep doing it, never to stop doing it. That must be beneficial. How to Get Rid of Glamour

We all know we have to detach from matter. We also have to detach from spirit. What steps are to be taken in this direction?

To detach from spirit is the easiest thing to do. We all know we have to detach from matter, we do not know how to do that. But to detach from spirit is so easy. You do what you like: if you want you can make a lot of money, millions, and with those millions you can make more millions, you can invest in the stock exchange, and so on. That is how to detach yourself from spirit.

The idea of matter is something which we can grasp, but the idea of spirit is more difficult to grasp. So what do we do? We put round it a coloured light. It becomes part of our ability to visualize. We can visualize a great spiritual ideal. This is our emotional body working on our idea of spirit. We see spirit as unobtainable or, if attainable, a tenuous attainment only can be had. We think of it as an ideal. It is us at our very best. We have the idea that God is watching us all the time. When we are alone perhaps we have a spiritual experience: we do not want to steal someone else's money. We do not feel envious or avaricious, we feel complete. There is nothing we want or need, we are just happy, joyfully happy, wanting nothing. Not wanting to be good, thinking: "I must be good." It is something which is done without effort, and being without effort we are in spirit and do not have to grasp for it.

By attaching to spirit, it is wanting it, grasping it, so it is not a detached view of spirit any more than a detached view of matter. It is learning to be yourself utterly without any needs, desires, without any wants at all, either of a spiritual or of a material nature. When we have that, we have the right walking between the pairs of opposites. It is not something we give up, it is something we do not encroach on because it is a given state, a very simple state. Few people can be simple enough not to want something: to be fed, nourished, to be liked or loved, to be looked up to, admired. Most want something from every situation. Just to be happy in Being is a wonderful state, a non-attached state. Not attached to spirit, because we are not seeking it, we would never dream of calling this a spiritual state, it is just being happy like a child is happy playing with toys, making sandcastles, without thinking about himself, when totally absorbed. Complete bliss, concentration in the moment, that is how to walk between the pairs of opposites.

CONFLICT

What is the role of conflict in relation to group work, group initiation? Where do you draw the line between good and bad conflict?

There is really no bad conflict but there is no good conflict either. Life provides you with the conflict whether you like it or not and so if life provides it, it is neither good nor bad, it is life, we've got a life, *c'est la vie.* That kind of conflict has no value in the sense of being good or bad. It is simply something with which we have to deal. The conflict which is 'bad' is the conflict which we create from our 'bad' actions, our hatred, our violence, our distaste for certain individuals; whatever it is, we create conflict. We all do this, of course, over and over again, all day long, all the time. That is not the kind of conflict I am talking about.

93

That conflict is 'bad', but it is not the conflict which is the fire of the evolutionary process. That is provided by life simply because we are part of life, we are souls in incarnation. We are living on the lower slopes of, say, Mount Etna. We know Mount Etna is a live volcano, we know it is going to erupt, sometime. We know that, sooner or later, lava will pour down and we only hope that our family will escape in time. Sometimes that happens, sometimes we are caught unawares. Whichever it is, it is something over which we have no control. Life provides us with this event which gives us conflict. A hurricane appears out of the blue, and there is nothing we can do to stop it. It is part of physical-plane life. That produces conflict, anxiety, disharmony, and of course destruction. But that is life, it is not something we have created.

Mr Bush, the US President, has created enormous conflict and anxiety in the last few months over whether to attack Iraq or not. He wants to attack Iraq and he is probably going to attack, whatever anybody says. He has created a huge cauldron of disharmony in the world which is now part of his karma. He has created it, but it need not be, that is not part of life.

For us, now, of course, it is part of our life. We can choose how to deal with it, but since we are citizens of countries these conflicts become part of the conflict of life for us. We have no personal karmic responsibility because we did not set this conflict in motion. But, depending on our viewpoint, whether we are for or against war, we contribute to this conflict. If we think, well, Saddam Hussein is an evil man (which I have no doubt he is), it is a good thing if the Americans get him off our backs, let them do it – that must be the point of view of very many people. If you think it is a good thing you are contributing to the conflict which he is setting in motion.

So it depends what we mean by conflict. If we have set it in motion it is our conflict, and we suffer the consequences. If it is part of the conflict of life, it provides the fire of the evolutionary process, through the great ray, Harmony through Conflict.

What is the role of conflict in relation to group work? The conflict which the group can resolve, which are the conflicts of life, are beneficial to the group and they can best be resolved, I would suggest, by treading carefully the line between the pairs of opposites, not attaching oneself to spirit or matter, moving between the two in the most detached way.

Could you say more about what you mean by the middle way?

It is not really a term I use, but it was used by the Buddha, which is good enough for me. The middle way is essentially about detachment. It is the way in which everything we do we see from the point of view of limits, of decorum, of non-excess, so we do not go too far in one direction or another. It is the way of tolerance, the non-fanatical way. It sees fanaticism as ugly and obstructive of the path. The middle way is the way which is tolerant, discriminating, and has a sense of proportion.

It is not the middle way if it is intolerant of opposites, or sees everything in black and white and in total opposition. The middle way sees like where there is like, and opposites where there are opposites, but without taking anything too far. The middle way is the path of sanity, the path, above all, of detachment and a sense of proportion.

We have noticed that when we are in conflict, if we detach, the pairs of opposites resolve. Why is the detachment so difficult?

The detachment is difficult because we are immersed in matter. If the soul was completely expressing itself through the matter, the opposite pole, we would not find it difficult to detach. It would be automatic because the soul is totally detached. It is filled with the love of God. It comes into incarnation to carry out the Plan of evolution. But it is not attached to anything.

95

The soul has no sense of time. It is in no hurry; it is not pushing us.

However, there are ways and means for the soul to push and occasionally it does. It may give its vehicle a life of severe inhibition, either physically, emotionally, or mentally, or all three. Why would a soul manifest through such a body? Barring the fact of accidents, which do happen at birth, the soul might give itself such a body because there had been a succession of lives in which the person made little or no progress. The soul might inhibit the progress until the person had worked out the karma. The soul might then come back into a life where it made a great advance. A physical-plane life of extreme limitation caused by illness, disease or malfunction can be a prelude to a great advance.

Why is it so difficult to be detached? It is difficult because it is difficult. If it were easy, everybody would do it. It is not easy because people are attached – everyone is attached. We are attached to the physical body that we can see: we identify with it, we want to preserve it. The instinct for self-preservation is very strong. It is the number one instinct to preserve the body, so we do not walk out from the pavement in front of a car or bus. The instinct for self-preservation has to be very strong, otherwise there would be no life.

We also take our emotions seriously. We think they are real, but they are not. Every emotion we have is the result of a glamour, a fantasy. It is just like a dream. Much of the time asleep we are dreaming. Then we wake up and say: "Oh, thank God. That was terrible. I am glad it was just a dream." We made it up. It is all symbolic. It relates to some fears or situations in our everyday life. If it is very compelling, we dream it again and again, perhaps all through life. It is nothing but a symbolic re-enactment of something that is troubling us, that has troubled us perhaps from childhood, that we have not been able to cope with in growing up, that our mother or father did or did not do, some trauma. Or dreams can result from events in the everyday world that annoyed us, that made us angry or sad, or feel self-pity.

All these emotions are unreal. When they get into our dreams they are as unreal as if they were the emotion itself. We give them to ourselves because of the thought-forming faculty of the human mind. It is only in deep sleep that the lower mind is really at rest, otherwise it is active to a greater or lesser extent. The closer we are to waking, the more active the lower mind becomes, with the most intense dreams just before we wake up.

People take their dreams and their emotions seriously. They think that they have to have them. We do not have to have any of our emotions. The feeling of the heart is a completely different thing from the emotions of the astral/emotional body. The emotions create the glamour which is such a heavy weight on humanity. But we do not have to be attached. We can detach. That is what evolution is about.

As soon as we get to 1.5 to 1.6 degrees initiate, we begin to find that what seemed impossible when we were 1.2 or 1.3 becomes easier to deal with. We feel the emotions, but they will not overtake us so much and so often. We will still have them, but they will lose their intensity, and we will find that we can detach from them in a very simple way. Just ask: "Who is this emotion happening to? To me. Who am I?" As soon as we ask: "Who am I?" we shift the point of identification and make a space between us and the experience of the emotion. If we do that constantly and conscientiously with everything that conjures up an emotion, we find that we can distance ourselves from them. They have no effect, or, if they do, it is only for a few minutes. They do not rule our life any more.

The astral plane is the seat of consciousness of the person who is astrally polarized. If they are gifted with astral imagination, the problems increase – and we have all the books that decorate the shelves of the esoteric bookstores, the astral nonsense that is put out as wisdom and experience by thousands of people.

What is of value is what is real, and that is only attainable when we are detached. If we look at something when we are detached, we get a completely different experience of it. When we are attached we see it totally subjectively; we take from it what we want. We want to be pleased, so we take what pleases us, makes us feel better.

If we look at it with detachment we would see, perhaps, that it has nothing to do with us, is of no value to us. It is not necessarily unreal, but of no value to us. What we have to do is learn to work more objectively, more in connection with the Plan of evolution which is directing the whole thing. We have free will but the trick is to adapt our free will to the Will of God. I sound like a clergyman! When I say God, I do not mean an old man with a beard. I mean the laws which are God, the Heavenly Man, and the laws which He has set into motion which create our planet. If we see objectively His line of action, meaning His Plan, His awareness of what may be or what can be, and seek to carry that out objectively as something which we feel equipped to do, then it is a very different story from looking at it subjectively.

In terms of conflict, how do you view wars?

We have to know that wars are bad and unnecessary. When they occur they act as part of the conflict which drives evolution. However, there can be all sorts of conflict without war, which is conflict carried to excess, the desire of some groups to get rid of groups that think differently. Or it may be simply the quickest way to take all for oneself, just to get rid of the opposition. The point is that modern weapons are so destructive that war has now become a major threat to the continued existence of the human race.

Conflict is ordinarily considered bad in society, but really it is a sign of aliveness if it can spark the necessary communication or dialogue to effect change. Conflict is a process that can lead to harmony. However, military conflict – lack of dialogue – cannot succeed. I believe everyone loses in modern war.

How true. The question is, conflict is ordinarily considered bad, but people take too narrow a view of conflict. Conflict is really the battleground of our life. There does not have to be war. We do not have to obliterate our enemy. We do not even have to have an enemy to have conflict. Just by being a soul in incarnation, there is enough conflict in that situation to give the fire to drive us forward in evolution.

If we have the aspiration which drives us upwards towards a higher state of ourselves and the life, conflict need not mean war. Of course, it often does where humanity is concerned. It is still an easy thing to go to war for the wrong reasons. If we are invaded by another nation, war is almost inevitable. We have to repel the invader. We call up the army, and hope that they will win and that the invader will go back home.

The trouble here in the US is that you have this huge country, America, and the 'Twin Towers' in New York were destroyed by terrorists on 9/11. Some 3,000 people lost their lives, which is indeed a tragedy, and dramatic in the way it happened, but you react as if the whole of America had been invaded by another nation. So you have to have a war against the invader, whom you call Terrorism, against Afghanistan, Iraq . . . and others? Terrorism is looked on as an invader in this country. You have to get it into proportion. Terrorism is worldwide. And you have to acknowledge the cause of terrorism.

If you are living in Britain, Spain or other countries, where bombs have been going off regularly for years, you do not like it, and people get killed. The IRA bombings went on for years in places like Belfast, which were devastated by terrorists.

London, Manchester and Birmingham also came under bombing attacks, but we just had to get on with life, meantime trying to make peace with the perpetrators, which hopefully, it would seem, is finally beginning to happen.

The British did not bomb Ireland because the Irish Republican Army were bombing Britain, nor did the UK bomb America because most of the funding of the IRA came, and still comes, from American Irish. If the logic of your government is that anyone who 'protects' terrorism is open ground for bombing, then the UK should have bombed Ireland and America long ago.

What I am trying to say is that conflict need not be war. We tend to think of conflict in terms of war. Certainly the Master talked about violence and hatred, and violence and hatred is conflict. Drug-running, crime, all of that is violence and creates hatred, separating societies, those who have, those who have not, the "rich parading their wealth before the poor", as Maitreya puts it. That creates conflict. That is something which this country has never awakened to.

The domination of the world society through investment and globalization is conflict-producing. It does not have to be a terrorist outrage like 11 September. It produces the conflict which results in pain and suffering of one group at the hands of another. We have to see conflict in the broadest terms, not only in terms of warfare. Anything that produces disharmony, discord and hatred, and the opposite of goodwill, is conflict.

All of these events, because we are souls in matter, produce the fire that drives us quickly forward along the evolutionary path. If we could start from the beginning and progress directly, detached all the way, we would progress without conflict and would create harmony. We do not have to have the conflict. Harmony through conflict: that is the result of the ray, but the harmony is possible theoretically. Of course, it does not happen because few are already at a point where they are unaffected by the disharmony.

Today it seems our world is in crisis, with the pairs of opposites never clearer: gross materialism and abject poverty. Maitreya's Sword of Cleavage forces humanity to make a choice – we must share or die. Can you comment on this?

People do not understand the saying in the Bible: "I come not to bring peace but a sword [the Sword of Cleavage]. I will set men against men, sons against fathers, brother against brother." It is a symbolic way of stating a great fact, that humanity does not see the best way to go, because it has no judgement, no tolerance, is badly educated, and so it tends to go the wrong way – not every time, of course, but as often as not. It ends up in calamity and war. If humanity knew the way, there would be conflict of course, but it would not necessarily lead to war and mass destruction.

The Sword of Cleavage, curiously enough, is the reality, but maybe not the one you expect. The Sword of Cleavage is really the energy of love. The energy of love is the sword which creates cleavage in the world. Cleavage is difference, separation, and yet, when we understand it, that energy is released to the world by Maitreya Who is the Avatar of Love. He releases that love in the world and it stimulates everybody without exception, the good, the bad, the altruistic, the selfish, the greedy, the unselfish, and so on. Everybody is stimulated. The energy itself is purely impersonal, it is neither good nor bad. It is an energy which stimulates, it brings together all peoples, and even the particles of matter which hold the world together. The particles of matter in our body are held together by that same energy. It is God the Son, the Christ aspect, the Consciousness aspect. That energy of love holds and binds together the particles of matter without which there would be no world, and when it is released in a mass way, as it has been for many years, it creates the Sword of Cleavage.

It stimulates the good, and people look at the good and see the good, but it also stimulates the bad, and people look at the bad, and see the bad. It is a human trait to look at the bad and say: "You say the world is changing for the better, but I see nothing but war, and rumour of war, and new diseases, and people losing their jobs and immigrants coming from other countries and taking away our jobs, and everything is getting worse. There is no doubt about it. Everything is getting worse, more materialistic, there is corruption everywhere: look at Enron, Worldcom and so on, all this corruption oozing out from the big corporations. We see street crime, drug-taking, mounting all over the world. We cannot say the world is better. It must be worse."

For them it is worse because they only see the worst. But at the same time, if they would look with educated eyes they would see a new world, they would see differences: more tolerance, new ideas, people like Nelson Mandela released after 27 years in prison, the end of apartheid, the reunification of Germany, the division into autonomous states in the Soviet Union where 'unity' was imposed by an elite on the people of Russia. The world has dramatically changed. The Cold War is over. America and Russia are, maybe not friends, but friendly. They can talk together.

All of this is the action of the Law of Love. This creates the Sword of Cleavage so that humanity will see clearly what the choice is: do we share and recreate the world, make it possible for all people to live together in peace and plenty, *"where no man lacks; where no two days are alike; where the Joy of Brotherhood manifests through all men"*, as Maitreya said [Message No. 3]? Or do we continue with the corruption and misery and eventually see the annihilation of our world? That is the choice before humanity. Maitreya will emphasize this and people will see clearly. But people can see clearly even today. As far as Maitreya is concerned they are already seeing the choice which we have to make: between sharing and justice for everyone or a growing distance between peoples and a war which would destroy all life. That is the Sword of Cleavage.

The pairs of opposites have never been clearer: gross materialism, stock exchanges reeling because of overwhelming greed, and at the same time people dying in millions from starvation. Maitreya's Sword of Cleavage forces humanity to make a choice: to share or die. He states it clearly: *"Men must share or die. There is no other course."* When it dawns on us that we share or we die, of course we will accept to share and that will create the conditions in which all can live in peace.

Conflict highlights our glamours. Does it speed up the deglamourization process?

Conflict can speed up the deglamourization process by its pain, by the suffering. When humanity sees clearly that we can no longer have one-third of the world living in affluence and two-thirds living in abject poverty, when we can no longer support that glamour, things will change. We cannot go on like that. If we try to, it will destroy all life on the planet. That is perhaps the major reason why Maitreya is in the world now. If He had waited longer it might have been too late. You will find that His timing is perfect.

Would you please elucidate the difference between the concepts of solution versus resolution as a way of handling the conflict of the pairs of opposites?

It is not about solution, but resolution. We resolve the seeming dichotomy between spirit and matter as soon as we cease to see them as a duality, which only in a relative sense they are.

There is the monad and its spiritual reality, and there is the physical plane and its material reality. From the point of view of the monad, the physical plane is not a reality. It is a shadow, as on a cinema screen. We see what look like people, but we know they are not people. There is a silver screen, and we see projected on it a whole show of shadows. We see valleys and mountains and cowboys shooting each other. It seems real but is not. That is how the soul sees the physical plane.

It is not real to the soul, only relatively real. All the people are there, the trees and houses are all there, but the vision of the soul observing is that it is all one, all just one moving shadow play. It is like a play, not all that serious. However serious we take it to be, seen from the soul it would make us smile at the happenings because they are so fanciful. It is light and airy and unimportant, insubstantial. As we go higher there is less and less form, less substance, but more and more reality and meaning. Here we have dense form and trivial inner substance. From the higher planes, it looks insubstantial and unreal, but here it is very solid and real. The things that we see and touch and deal with, from locomotives to tanks, are real, big, heavy things. But from the point of view of the soul, it is all like a kind of game, a children's game that is being played, which has relatively little consequence.

What is of consequence on the soul plane is the reality of the Plan. The soul, without any hurry and not under any strain or stress, is involved in carrying out the Plan. It sees and knows the Plan, and is responsible for the actions of its vehicle to carry it out. We have free will on this level and often do not respond. We waste lives, which is a pity.

Returning to the question, to elucidate the difference between the concept of solution versus resolution, in nature there is no solution. There is resolution. There is bringing all conflict into a state of equilibrium. Nature creates equilibrium and every time the equilibrium is upset, it has to do something to re-establish it. That something might be a storm or a typhoon, but it re-establishes, not a solution, but a resolution of the disequilibrium. It is a creative process, unstable in a certain sense, but eternal. Yet it is continually changing as life is able to create a higher vehicle for its expression. It is a question of the life itself, and the vehicle through which it expresses itself. Evolution proceeds through the creation of more adequate vehicles for the expression of life. That is creativity. The essence of the Plan is that it is creative.

The pairs of opposites are there so we can recognize the way between them. Is this correct?

That is why they have been there from the very beginning! God said: "Those people around about the year 2002 are pretty smart, but not quite smart enough. They have to recognize the way between the pairs of opposites. So what will I do? I know. I will make pairs of opposites. We will have spirit, and we will have matter. We will bring them together and they will find their way between those two." That is it. The pairs of opposites are there so that we can recognize the way between them. Well, that is one way of putting it! Mystical!

Maitreya's priorities use this method of following the middle path between the pairs of opposites. For example, Maitreya said what is needed is to take the best of capitalism and the best of communism and synthesize them into one combined system.

He did not quite say that, but I know what you mean. He said that a cart does not go at all if it has only one wheel. You need two wheels: one wheel you can call capitalism, the other wheel you can call socialism. If it does not have the two, it will not go.

I have asked my Master about the relative balance between these two forces as making for the best kind of social democracy or democratic socialism, which Maitreya announced as the future method which would be adopted by the world, and which is largely adopted in most states in Europe. I asked Him the best proportion, and He said: "Well, what do you think?" I thought: "Say 30 per cent of capitalism and 70 per cent of socialism." He said: "Exactly that. That is what is best." Seventy per cent of socialism giving the method of dealing with the big socially dependent institutions like transport, power, water, and so on. And the icing on the cake, the luxuries, more or less, of life being the result of 30 per cent private enterprise.

ASPIRATION

The nature of aspiration could be described as the desire for betterment. How does aspiration relate to detachment? How can we aspire and be detached at the same time?

It depends on the level of our aspiration. Somebody who is 0.6 or 0.7 has aspiration to take the first initiation. Whatever he does will be relative to the degree from 0.6 to 1. Somebody who is already 1 will want to be, say, 1.5, 1.6 and becoming mentally polarized, or 2. If you are 1, why not aspire to 2? If you are 2, why not aspire to be 3? Aspiration itself changes, it depends on where we are, and on who is aspiring.

The person who is more or less dominated by his astral mechanism, if he is aspiring, will have an aspiration which will be not very detached. It will relate to his astral longings, which are unreal, but real for that person; from a higher point of view they are unreal. The aspiration is real so far as it goes, but it is not detached aspiration.

The more advanced aspiration of a more evolved individual will be relatively more detached. The more detached the person is, the purer will be the aspiration. The aspiration will not be self-oriented, it will be altruistic, soul-oriented and for the good of all. If we see it in terms of the aspiration of a person who is astrally polarized, that of someone who is mentally polarized and of a person who is spiritually polarized, we get three different kinds of aspiration. They will all be aspiration but there will be degrees of attachment. The astrally polarized will be looking for results of the aspiration, they will want it for a purpose. A person with mental aspiration will be more detached, and will have less of this longing for results, and the aspiration of the person with spiritual polarization will be totally pure and to do with the betterment of life for all people. It would be an aspiration for betterment without any personal attachment.

In the same way, Masters aspire, too. Is detachment for Them also an issue to take into account?

The Masters are totally detached, that is what makes Them Masters. If the Masters were attached to Their aspiration, They would not be Masters. It is the Master's awareness and control of the different planes that account for His detachment. He does not have the problem of detachment but I am sure He has other problems: of visualizing, becoming aware of what up till then He is unaware of, just as we do. We cannot imagine what we cannot imagine. He has a thousand ways and means of becoming aware which as yet we do not have.

Could you comment on the differences between idealization and aspiration?

Aspiration goes on right through life, through the Master's life, and on and on into eternity. It is a function of spirit to aspire to something else, something beyond; until we go beyond we do not know that there is a beyond. If we limit consciousness, the source, what we call God, to what we can imagine of God then we are bringing God down to practically nothing, because we cannot imagine, with the greatest effort, the nature of God. We have seen the Love of God, we have seen the Wisdom of God, we have not seen the Will of God. Can we imagine the Will of God? Do we know what the Will of God is? The Will is the Purpose. The Buddha showed the Wisdom of God, Maitreya showed the Love of God through Jesus. Maitreya today will show the Wisdom, the Love and the Will of God. That is the new revelation which Maitreya brings. The Will of God is something which humanity has barely thought about as yet. We think it is to do with what happens when there is a hurricane or a volcanic eruption. We say it is "the Will of God", but it is nothing to do with the Will of God. The Will of God is something completely different. I will leave it to Maitreya to outline eventually the Purpose of God. At the core of our existence lies a tremendous secret which is the Purpose of Life, the Purpose of God. That is what Maitreya this time brings to the world.

Idealization is the capacity of the human mind to idealize, to visualize an as yet non-existing state, and that is not the same thing as aspiration. The ability to idealize, or to ideate, is closely tied up with the quality of aspiration but it depends on the level, as I said before. The idealization of a person who is astrally polarized is different from one who is mentally polarized, and different again from one who is spiritually polarized. We have to take all that into account.

What is the difference between aspiration and instinct in animals?

Aspiration and instinct are not quite the same. They are related, of course. Flocks of birds in flight are guided by instinct and by the use of certain factors like the position of the sun, which they remember by instinct. The older ones teach the young ones, and they follow by instinct, and so are able to navigate the globe. That is instinct, but that is not the same as aspiration. Animals and creatures evolve through instinct, which is below the threshold of consciousness. The aspiration of a fish to come out of the sea and become a mammal is aspiration, although at that level it functions like a kind of instinct. It aspires towards a higher function, a higher mobility. Flying is one of those dreams that humanity has because we know that we are really immaterial. We are in a material body, but essentially are weightless. It is an aspiration towards lightness, towards the quality of light itself, the quality of life without the form. It is a recognition that the true nature of life is outside form.

Form makes life visible; we recognize life by its impact on our lives through form. Everyone has dreamed that there is a quality of life in which there is no form. There is consciousness but no form. There are colossal Lives in our own solar system Who carry out activity of tremendous value and creativity, Who have no form whatsoever. We recognize only that which has form because we have limited vision.

In the first race, the Lemurian, humanity had to develop the physical body. Now we move, act, run without thinking about it. That is below the threshold of conscious action. On the mental plane we are working with ideas, ratiocination. Our science is built on the understanding of the laws governing that level of thought. On those levels we know that we can think, build computers, spacecraft, and we know that if we do the right thing, the spacecraft will go around the moon or Mars, and can be brought back to Earth. We are confident that we can do that. It is using the concrete mind to create artefacts, knowing that they will do the job successfully.

There is a level of consciousness which does not use ratiocination and calculation. There is a much more abstract quality – intuition – which comes from the soul. The next race will not think as we think but will use intuition. The more advanced people of this race are already using intuition to some extent. We use the term 'intuition' very loosely. We see it as a function of the mind, whereas it comes from the buddhic level of consciousness, the soul.

It is reflected on the still astral plane, it is knowing without knowing, without even thinking. We know because we know because we know. At present we have to use both our rational mind and what we would call an intuitive mind. Eventually the thinking, rational mind, the computer, will drop below the threshold of consciousness, and we will intuit immediately and know the answer without thinking about it.

Can you comment on the relationship between desire and aspiration, and about complacency and aspiration? What is happening there? Is there a lack of friction with people who are complacent?

Aspiration is desire, but desire is oriented to the self and aspiration is not. It is oriented to a new state, a liberated, a better state, something above the present. It is not self-oriented like: "I desire to be a better this or to be a that." That would be desire. Aspiration is an abstract longing for a better state of Being, not to do with this individual. The individual has the desire, but the detached individual has the aspiration. That is the essence of the spirituality of the detached individual.

There is a goal involved, right?

The 6th ray of Idealism dominates the life of America. America lives through its personality vehicle. That is the reality today. The desire principle is extremely powerful as it is expressed through the American people: the desire for wealth, for money, for control, the desire to be the best and biggest, to win. All of that is personality desire. The aspiration of the soul of America, which is 2nd-ray, is quite different: it is to serve the world, to help, to make it a better place. It is given little scope because the personality is so powerful, so all-pervading, that the soul aspect is only now and again expressed, as, for instance, in the Marshall Plan [the 'European Recovery Programme', US economic aid for the reconstruction of Europe after World War II].

The world, as DK put it, is waiting for the soul aspect of America to manifest. When it does, it will take up the Christ's ideas and, as quickly as it possibly can, will put them into effect from its personality. The soul will give it the vision and spiritual vitality to do it, but the desire to still be the best, to give the best to the world, better than anybody has ever given, the most beautiful freedom, the best justice that has ever been, that ambition comes from the personality. You will see.

America will be the one who makes the biggest sacrifices for the sake of the environment. From saying: "No, we will have nothing to do with it (the Kyoto Protocol), it is un-American, it is against American interest," the very opposite will be the case. When the 2nd ray of America takes up the ideas of Maitreya and seeks to put them into effect, it will do it through its 6th-ray personality, and it will be the best at doing it. You will see: sooner, quicker, bigger, better.

LAW OF CAUSE AND EFFECT

What is the relation between the Law of Cause and Effect and the resolution of the pairs of opposites?

The Law of Cause and Effect affects us so long as we are creating karma. The karma is the result of our response to the conflict which arises in everybody's life, which drives us forward and gives us the fire to produce the resolution. If we are – as the Master states we are, and all esoteric teaching agrees – souls in incarnation, we are spirit and matter in fused relationship. We have the problems arising out of that

111

confluence of spirit and matter: action, movement, radiation, truth and beauty; and the opposite: inert, unresponsive matter and low vibration. The task is to evolve to the point where these two are totally reconciled and the spirit relates to, and is demonstrated by, the man or woman on the physical plane.

Up to a certain point that is done through the response to the action of cause and effect. The more we are ruled by the Law of Cause and Effect – that is, the more we do what we do just because we like doing it, because it satisfies us, because it is the path of least resistance – the more we create karma. We cannot avoid it. We set in motion causes, the effects stemming from which make our life. Every life is made in that way, is the result of the action of karma.

There is, of course, personal karma, group karma, national karma and world karma. We are subject to all of these karmas. I am talking about personal karma, set in motion by one's own actions. Karma has a very powerful effect until we can begin to resolve the pairs of opposites, grow more detached in our actions and so create fewer effects.

Suffering is the result of violation of the law, but it is also born out of the very nature of the relationship of spirit to matter. That is why we suffer, why we have pain, why we need the law of karma to establish, as always, a new equilibrium. We upset the equilibrium of the law and as we upset it, it produces an effect. These effects cause a reaction from the law of karma to set in motion action which eventually, sooner or later, causes that disturbance to be brought into equilibrium again by our suffering, pain, illness, whatever it happens to be.

If we act against the law, knowingly or unknowingly, we create a disturbance in that cohesion of equilibrium that necessitates an action of karma to re-establish the equilibrium. If we have killed someone, then, sooner or later, we get killed. If we bring pain or suffering on people, then, sooner or later, we receive that degree of pain or suffering in equal measure.

The natural law of the nature of Beingness itself creates the necessity to re-establish the equilibrium which we have upset.

The more advanced we become, the less the Law of Cause and Effect, or karma, acts, because we are detached. If you are detached you do not create karma. The karma is created from the attachment to the physical body, or the emotional/astral body or the mental body; it is the result of these attachments, the belief that what we think or dream or imagine is real; it is the inability of humanity to see reality, to see only an illusion until that illusion is gradually dispersed and we see clearly. When we see clearly, and act therefore more correctly, we make fewer karmic reactions and so life becomes easier.

Is it accurate to say that karma and glamour are the only things that prevent us from Self-realization?

My quick answer to that would be no, it is not accurate to say that. What else prevents us from Self-realization? Ourselves, we do it. The fact that we are in matter creates karma. That creates the glamour, the conflicts, and thus creates the fire that generates the energy for evolution. At the same time, while we are in the midst of that conflict, we are producing both glamour and negative karma.

The Master DK wrote (through Alice A. Bailey) that more good karma is created than bad karma. Can you imagine? This rotten old world with its corrupt political systems is creating less bad karma than good karma. What prevents Self-realization is the inertia of the disciple – in the first place, the inertia of the matter of our bodies. These bodies are created by tiny, devic lives. Every atom is a little life which is carrying out its own evolution by becoming part of the body of the human evolution. It is gradually preparing itself to become, eventually, a human being.

Everything in life in the whole of cosmos is on the way to becoming human, is human or has gone on beyond the human.

We are the midway point, the meeting point of spirit and matter. That is the problem, the challenge, and the tremendous experience for us, that we provide the exact point of confluence between spirit and matter that makes evolution possible. The conditions – the conflict and the violence – which we create in the meantime are the glamours arising from the discrepancy in vibration between the spiritual reality which we are and the matter of which our physical, astral and mental bodies are constructed. Each of these bodies is made up of tiny devic or angelic lives. The glamours are overcome as we begin to control their activity, which has a self-oriented purpose. As long as they are in charge, the matter remains matter. When the control comes from the energy of the soul, we gradually change the condition of the atomic matter, and gain control of the path of evolution. This is why it is so important to realize the non-duality of the pairs of opposites, treading the path between them, not of avoidance, but of non-attachment.

This is the path of initiation. The bodies are gradually being transformed by the soul. Self-realization comes near as we gradually pass from one initiation to the next. Each initiation brings a higher frequency to bear on the devic lives making up the atomic structure of the physical, astral and mental bodies. The atomic structure is gradually changed, and changes the activity of these devic lives. They are no longer in charge of the process. They feed our bodies with their impulses, but the energy from the soul begins to take charge. The personality becomes more in control of the physical body, which begins to respond to instruction from the mental plane. The astral body, too, begins to 'cool down' and become calm. Essentially, the astral body should be, and in an evolutionary sense will become, like a still lake, no longer sweeping the individual with its emotions. It then acts like a mirror for the buddhic level of consciousness. The buddhic is the second level of the Spiritual Triad, which brings in the will, the love/wisdom and the intelligence of the soul. The buddhic consciousness, reflected on that still lake, we experience as intuition.

The tiny devic lives on the astral plane are more or less in control until about 1.5 to 1.6 degrees of initiation when mental polarization begins. After that they gradually become less imposing on the life of the individual. It does not mean that we do not have emotions, but we are not swept or overwhelmed by them so much. We learn to detach from the impact of their activity on the astral body. The soul energy is so much higher than that of the material body, in this case the astral, that we gradually gain control of the astral plane. That is not complete by any means until 2.5 to 2.6, at which point spiritual polarization begins.

The devic life from our point of view is the life of matter. From their point of view, it is a completely conscious life. It is like the cells of our body which have their own existence apart from our mental consciousness, and carry out their actions according to our DNA and the amount of vitamins, minerals and food extracts we give them to eat and drink. If we bring enough of the soul energy to bear, we begin to control them.

As well as karma, it is our capacity to change the quality of the life of our vehicles that determines when we achieve Self-realization. We are in charge, or the devas are in charge. But the great magnet that we call Life, which is driving the whole of evolution forward, sooner or later is too strong for any group or individual to withstand, and we are driven forward, willy-nilly. We may not make Self-realization at this stage, but eventually we will come to that point.

It is not glamour or karma alone that prevents Self-realization, but the amount of karma and the density of the glamour will depend on the degree of control which people have or do not have over their vehicles.

How does karma work?

Karma is the main law governing life in our solar system. By the functioning of that law every thought, every action, sets into motion a cause or causes. The effects stemming from these causes make our lives for good or ill. It is all-powerful and truly good. The law of karma seeks to arrive at a point of equilibrium. That, essentially, is what karma is, the achieving of equilibrium. If we set into motion causes whose effects make for conflict, violence, discord, pain, suffering and evil, then, inevitably, to create equilibrium, they have to be resolved. They are resolved by ourselves who created them. We receive it back. It comes to us and we say: "Oh, I had a terrible time, what an unlucky year it has been." It is all the resolution of past karma. It may not be the immediate past, it could be lives past.

The Master DK also wrote that nobody receives more karma of a negative nature than they can cope with. Not everyone would agree with that, especially people who commit suicide, because they cannot face the karma of their actions, or cannot face life for various reasons. They could say: "No, life is just impossible. I do not want to go on living," not knowing what is around the corner. This is why suicide is never a clever or intelligent way out because we never know what is around the corner. We cannot tell how it might all open up and be blissful for the next 20 years, a kind of bliss that we could not even begin to hope for. From the resolution of the karma which we find so heavy today can come the bliss, ease, painlessness, the 'good' karma, as we call it, of succeeding years.

Karma is not the carrying out of the command of God: "An eye for an eye and a tooth for a tooth." That is the law of karma put in the most negative way, the way of the past. God, or what we call God – whether that be the God of our planet, the Heavenly Man, or the God of our solar system, the Solar Logos – is essentially good. That goodness pervades every aspect of karma even if we feel it to be negative and painful in the extreme. It is aiming at the establishment of harmony and equilibrium – above all equilibrium – where the energies are balanced in exact degree to the causes which set them in motion.

Do our past actions make our future experiences inevitable?

Our future experiences are inevitable in that they are the re-establishing of equilibrium if we have done something against the Law of Harmlessness.

Can one eliminate karma through service and changes in consciousness?

Yes. Karma can drop away as we learn to live according to the Plan. We do not make bad karma if we do not make bad actions. If we do not steal and bomb poor countries and things like that, then we do not make negative karma. Hence the need for harmlessness in all our actions; individually, nationally and internationally.

If, for example, we know that the Plan of evolution is that we live together in peace and harmony, sharing the resources of the planet which are provided for all and, as a result, there is harmony, justice and freedom everywhere, we can be certain that the lives of all will go forward according to the law. Our lives will be good, fruitful, creative and splendid in every sense of the word.

When we create conflict, violence, hatred, injustice and oppression, we create negative karma. We are no longer working within the Plan of God. The Plan of God is a reality. In biblical terms it is so vague, so mystical, but in esoteric terms it is absolutely practical. Esotericism is the most practical science or philosophy. Through service, and the changes of consciousness which ensue, we burn up karma.

By changing ourselves, we change the nature of the karma we create, and can deal more potently with the karma of the past.

SPIRITUALIZING MATTER

You have said that the soul is perfect at its own level. Then why does it need to go through this evolutionary process to evolve?

The soul at its own level is a perfect reflection of the Heavenly Man, the God of our planet. It needs no higher evolution on this planet. It is the soul in incarnation which needs perfection. It comes into incarnation as a sacrifice; its own self-sacrificial will impels it into incarnation to carry out the Plan of the Logos.

How do we spiritualize matter?

By spiritualizing the matter of our own bodies in the first place. As a race we spiritualize the animal, vegetable and the mineral kingdoms by the radiation of our soul energy. The secret of transformation from lower to higher is done through radiation. That is why at the edge of the first kingdom, the mineral, we have radioactive matter. Radioactivity is the nature of the boundary of the mineral and vegetable kingdoms. Radiation is the link which makes vegetation possible.

As the vegetable kingdom evolves it forms, by radiation, a link with the animal kingdom. The radioactivity of the vegetable kingdom rests in the perfumes and colours of flowers, for instance. All those wonderful colours and the marvellous perfumes are energy radiations. At the very edge of the vegetable kingdom some plants eat insects, and thus lead into the animal kingdom.

The animal kingdom evolves, and eventually forms a body for the next kingdom, the human kingdom. We owe our physical body to the animal kingdom but we are not animals.

We are the next kingdom, which develops by the radiation of mind. The mind is a radiatory faculty, and makes possible the evolution of humanity. As we radiate more and more, we go through the initiatory process. At every initiation we receive a higher vibration of energy, thus becoming more magnetic, attracting more matter of a subatomic quality into our bodies, which gradually change into the body of light of a Master. When we take the fifth initiation, we are a Master; our bodies are made entirely of light.

We have always been that light; we return to it, but in total consciousness. That is the work of the soul as the Divine Intermediary between the spiritual and the physical levels. The soul makes spiritualization of matter possible. This spiritualizing of matter proceeds through all the kingdoms until the planet is perfected in terms of the Plan in the mind of the Planetary Logos. At every initiation we are shown a part of the Plan. We have a deeper insight into the Plan and of our part in it. That is what initiation is really about. It stabilizes the degree of radiation reached, and the amount of light, therefore, which is in the bodies of the initiate at each initiation.

Does spiritualizing matter necessarily involve conflict?

As we work with the purpose of spiritualizing matter, inevitably we are dealing with conflict because we are wrapped up in matter. The soul has no conflict, it does not know the meaning of conflict. The conflict is the result of the massive difference in vibrational terms of the soul on its plane and of the matter of the material planes into which it has incarnated. So there is always a conflict.

Matter has its own integral needs and where these are satisfied there is no conflict. Where, for instance, the physical body demands more than it needs (and we allow our physical body to demand more than it needs – DK has said that most people eat four times more than they need), then of course it creates conflict which manifests as ill-health. On the physical plane we can see the direct result of conflict of a material kind. Spiritualizing of matter occurs without our necessarily being aware of the conflict, but we are in it, it arises at every moment, everything we do in life creates a conflict with the soul which we are. We are always creating actions, karmic results, as a personality, imbued with the soul but still unable to manifest to any great extent the qualities of the soul. That is where the conflict arises. Matter itself does not have conflict, nor does spirit itself have conflict. It is when the two are linked together and the matter is trying to become spirit that the conflict arises.

It is the result of bringing a very high level of vibration, the soul energy, into matter that the conflict arises. The soul knows that it will take thousands of incarnations for the person to change sufficiently, and it does this by a long, drawn-out war.

Conflict is a war between the personality and the soul and it starts as soon as the person 'awakens', when the Christ Principle is born in the cave of the heart (the heart at the right side of the chest, the seat of the soul in the etheric-physical body). When the soul light is awakened in that centre, the person begins on 'the path of return', a return to the spirit, because the soul is the spirit. When we say return, it is not as if we are going back anywhere. It is that the soul is able more and more to manifest through its vehicle. Until that time the vehicle is too inert. There is tamas and rajas; rajas is fiery power, light, and tamas is inertia, lack of movement, lack of light. So we have these two opposing forces. Interestingly, the 4th ray, which I think is the key to the handling of these pairs of opposites, is the ray in which the tamasic, the inertia aspect, and the rajasic, the fiery aspect, are curiously equal, and that is a great problem for the 4th-ray type. He has to find the way to walk between the two.

Sometimes he is full of fire and can quickly be inspired by a great cause, can be fired up, inspired. The 4th-ray individual can do anything when he is charged up in that way. When that is not called for, he often has the inertia of the other, the matter aspect. These two are strangely equal in this type and the secret for him – and I think the secret for all Beings in relation to this resolving of the pairs of opposites – is to tread carefully the path between the two, not identifying with one or the other but being perfectly detached.

You said the re-education of humanity is so important. How can we teach about the pairs of opposites and detachment?

You can explain that we are a spiritual kingdom, that the essence of life is spiritual and we are souls in incarnation. The soul incarnates in matter which at this level of our existence appears to us to be the opposite pole to the spirit aspect. It is, but only in a relative sense.

There is a gradation of matter in the relative amounts of atomic and subatomic particles it possesses. The spirit aspect is real on its level, and as it manifests on the physical plane it changes the quality of matter. Matter is the lowest aspect of spirit and spirit is the highest aspect of matter. As the matter aspect is spiritualized it returns gradually through the planes and is perfected in the process. That spiritualizing of matter is the human role in evolution. As souls, we have descended, immersed ourselves in matter. The soul creates bodies of matter – physical, astral and mental – and a personality which synthesizes all of these. A personality is, as it were, the sum total of all the personality expressions over aeons of time.

Humanity as a whole is reaching a point where, on a mass scale, the personality as a true reflection of the soul is being realized. The integration of the personality goes on apace and can better use the energy and the vehicles of the soul, creating finer vehicles, better able to transmit spiritual energy, to radiate more correctly and to become more knowledgeable. It is both a matter of achieving certain qualities and also the means of expressing these qualities, forging an instrument which is attuned to making it work.

You talk about the sacred heart or the spiritual heart of man. Is there really a practical way where we can experience that, feel that, and start at least to begin to know ourselves as souls?

The first thing is to know yourself as a soul. That is why the Christ Principle is born in the cave of the heart of the man or woman in incarnation. It is still matter, but in that matter is born the light and love of spirit. Very small in the beginning, it builds up and up and takes you to the first initiation. Finally it takes you to the fifth initiation. It is the same principle that takes you through the whole of the initiatory process to perfection, when the soul's work is done.

It is awakening to the fact that you are the soul. All the religions of the world have been formed to teach humanity, because all religion is a path to God. More or less distorted in how it describes the path, but properly understood religion is a method whereby the soul aspect of reality is shown to be what in fact we are. We are souls who have wrapped themselves in matter, taken incarnation, and are going through a process of return to the original state of pure spirit but with all the experience of having been in matter. By doing that the matter aspect of our planet is being perfected, spiritualized, all the time.

The aim, the role of humanity is to spiritualize matter. We do it in the first place through the spiritualization of our own body. We are bringing that matter up, stage by stage. Matter is essentially light, but it does not look like light while it is in form. We are showing that that form can become more and more rarefied, more and more light. More and more subatomic particles are drawn to those bodies – physical, astral, mental – throughout the evolutionary process, until in the end there is only light. A Master is a solid, physical person, as you will see, but His body is not subject to the laws of matter. It is subject only to the laws governing the light of our planet. He has conquered death. He has conquered the life of the physical plane. It is no longer real for Him, but it never was real, except relatively.

The reality is that there is only one whole. That whole has two poles, one we call spirit, the other matter. They are two parts of one totality, and each has the potential of the other. That is the secret of it. It is not as if everything is all spirit, and matter does not count. That has been the way of the last 2,000 years in which people have denied the reality of the physical body. It has been abhorrent to Christians throughout that time. They have hated and crucified it. Crucifixion is the chief symbol of Christendom, but it should be resurrection. Resurrection out of matter into spirit.

The Masters do not ignore the physical plane. Two-thirds of Them are in physical-plane bodies; that is how They appear on Earth. But They are not limited by the functions of the physical plane. They do not need to eat, or sleep, go to a shop, have a haircut or buy clothes. Whatever They need, They can think into existence. It is an understanding of the laws governing spirit and matter.

There is only spirit, fundamentally, but spirit is not only at one level, and the lowest we call matter. Spirit and matter are seen as one but are also distinct in the incarnational sense. They are brought into relation in order to do what cannot otherwise be done. We cannot spiritualize matter if we do not have matter. The body of this planet has to be perfected. This is a body of expression of a great cosmic Being, Who is on a path of perfectionment. One day, this world will be a shining orb in the heavens, radiating its beauty out for every telescope to see. That is because we are gradually perfecting it. We are spiritualizing it by our action as souls coming into incarnation.

Can an average person like us access the higher mind at any given moment?

An average person at our level could access the higher mind at given moments – for instance in meditation or in a very exalted state as a result of some blessing that might be conferred on one. It is possible, but not as a normal rule because we still have to understand and function through our own mental vehicle. We could be open to the stimulus of a blessing from a higher mind conferring on us a view of life more from the soul's point of view. That is perfectly possible.

Is that [accessing the higher mind] a reasonable approach to solving the problem of the pairs of opposites?

It has nothing to do with the pairs of opposites. The higher mind is the vehicle of the soul. We would only see that in relation to the pairs of opposites once the soul had taken incarnation, because the pairs of opposites only exist for a soul in incarnation. It is soul brought into fusion with matter that creates the pairs of opposites.

If you were to meditate and see the world as the soul sees the world, then that experience, if it happened strongly enough or frequently enough, would, for an intelligent person, help him or her to resolve the pairs of opposites. But at the end of the process they are not seen as being there at all. The pairs of opposites are an illusion. That is the point. But we have to go through the illusion before we know that it was an illusion. If we were to see things in the way the soul sees them, we would see them as an illusion. Whether that would help us or not depends on the individual.

THE DWELLER ON THE THRESHOLD

Can you explain the Dweller on the Threshold and how that is different from the ordinary experience of karma or conflict?

The Dweller on the Threshold is an accumulation from life to life by each individual of its faults, its wrongdoing, through all the incarnational cycles. That builds up into a personality. That is the lower aspect which the person has to be able to resolve – the dichotomy between the soul and its qualities of beauty, truth and love, and the Dweller on the Threshold which we become conscious of as the inherited evil, inadequacies, facility for creating faults and mistakes, in the life of humanity.

The Dweller on the Threshold is that which creates the glamour of our life. It hides the truth, the reality of our life, from our perception. It holds humanity enthralled and will go on doing so for a long time. It is that glamour which is overcome, to a degree, at the second initiation.

Between 1.5 or 1.6 and 2 we are meeting the Dweller on the Threshold over and over again. Every incarnation brings us to this same place where we are enthralled by our dreams, the misapprehensions, the visions which we mistake for the truth. That has to be overcome. We have to learn to see through all of that and see things as they are, simply as they are. They are always very different from how we imagine. Our own qualities are always different from how we imagine. What we think of as our best qualities are often our worst. What we think we can do is a figment of our astral imagination, a fantasy, yet we take it to be true.

Until we get through that phase and take the second initiation these are powerful brakes on our progress. They are powerful thoughtforms. The Dweller on the Threshold is a reality, the sum total of all our personality experiences, the creator of our karma, and it holds us back. Until we can see through that and become detached from all the glamour, the attachment to our dreams, our values, our sense of ourselves, our ambitions, hopes – until we are free of all of that, we are locked in the glamour.

When we take the third initiation we have brought the astral elemental under control and, at least to a sufficient degree, the mental elemental also. At the third initiation, which integrates the vehicles of all three bodies, they are vibrating at the same frequency. When this is achieved the soul can really take over the life of the individual.

From the viewpoint of the Masters, the third initiation is really the first initiation because it is the first true soul initiation. Then we can take up the tasks of the fourth and the fifth initiations, which might take another couple of lives or so. It can usually be done quickly from the third initiation, because the soul is working potently through the individual. The radiance of the soul is the magnetism of such an individual, and so we recognize it.

How do we know we are dealing with the Dweller on the Threshold as opposed to something else like a common, ordinary experience?

You do not. It is all done from consciousness. You are either dealing with it or not. You never give it a thought. You just become more and more detached. The thought never arises in you because you are detached.

So there is nothing extraordinary about the experience?

It is so gradual and, in a way, so logical. If you remove your attention from something, it no longer irritates you. If you are always thinking about the Dweller: "Oh, God, that Dweller," if you are going home and you go up the stairs and: "Oh, God, it is that Dweller again, standing there at the door!" take your mind off it; give yourself a chance. Learn to detach, and it will take care of itself.

Is it accurate to say that the Bhagavad Gita [Hindu scripture] is a symbolic representation of the soul's conflict in matter?

The short answer to that is yes. The Bhagavad Gita is really a dissertation by various Beings on the path of evolution as it mainly concerns the astral/emotional plane. It is about the nature and the overcoming of glamour. All of Shakespeare also is about glamour and the overcoming of glamour.

THE 4TH RAY

The 4th ray will be increasing in intensity in the next few decades. One would think that this is an opportunity to stimulate a greater point of tension for humanity globally and individually. Will this play an important role in producing initiation, and in which ways will it specifically affect humanity in relation to producing conflict?

It is true that in a few decades from now the 4th ray will come into incarnation as is the 7th ray now. These rays will work together. In Transmission Meditation, after the cosmic energies 1, 2 and 3 are released, the ray energies come in. The rays 4 and 7 are always the first to be brought in and together. The 4th ray produces harmony, harmonizing all the rays. The 7th ray is used to anchor them on the physical plane. The 7th ray is the most practical of all the rays in the sense that it relates the spiritual ideal to the physical plane. The ritual action of the 7th creates, through repetition, an energy which anchors the idea. The 6th ray has the ideal, and no difficulty in visualizing the ideal, but great difficulty in making the ideal manifest because it is not looking for manifestation; it is satisfied with the vision.

The 7th ray takes the vision and anchors it, brings it down to the physical plane by its action, by organization, by making it a fact. That means it knows how to organize, how to construct institutions, forms, through which the ideal can manifest. These two together, 4 and 7, besides making for the highest forms of art, according to the Masters, are really bringing the radiation that we call beauty into line with the radiation that we call ritual. These two forms of radiation will be brought together and create a tremendous new awakening on the part of humanity.

People will become altogether more creative, not only in painting and other art, but beyond art. The art of living will become highly important to humanity, who will become more and more creative. Not that we need lots of different ways of living, but the art of living together in peace, safely, securely, in harmony, is the art of living, doing what we do in harmony, according to the Law, the Law of the ray and the Law of the Logos.

How does the release of the Shamballa force during the past three decades contribute to the level of conflict for humanity? And how does this differ from the 4th-ray influence?

The level of conflict and disharmony is raised by the outflow of the Shamballa force, but that is outweighed by the benefits which it has also contributed because the 1st ray is the ray of Will or Purpose. It is the Purpose of the Logos which is being carried out. The Shamballa force embodies that Purpose, and the Will brings the purpose into being. Harmony, love and goodwill is manifested by the action of the Shamballa force. In its initial impact on the lower strata of society it can have what we would call a negative effect. It stimulates degrees of violence but that is temporary and outweighed by the benefits; otherwise it would not be released.

In the release of any great energy, there is a double action. One which is, sooner or later, beneficial, and one which is immediately, for a short time, detrimental, but which is quickly overcome by the benefits conferred on a much wider scale over other members of society.

The same might be said of the energy of love. The energy of love is absolutely neutral. It is neither 'good' nor 'bad'. We think of love as being all good. It is neutral. It is the 'Sword of Cleavage' which is used by the Christ deliberately to stimulate all Beings. It stimulates the good and the bad. It stimulates the selfish and greedy, and at the same time the altruism of others.

It creates a line down the middle so humanity can see where it has to stand, with no blurred edges, just where is the good and where is the evil, where the greed and where the true soul altruism.

There are people who pretend to themselves that they are selfless and all for the good of the world. But at the basis of their life they are greedy and selfish. The Sword of Cleavage cuts through this hypocrisy, and shows people in their true light. So we can see clearly that if we go one way, it will make for total disaster. If we go another, it will make for the generation of a new world. This is the road humanity has to choose, and pray that it does.

PART THREE

ILLUSION

*This chapter is based on an edited version of a talk given by Benjamin Creme at the Transmission Meditation Conference held near San Francisco, USA, in August 2003. (First published in **Share International** magazine, January/February 2004.)*

In the Alice Bailey books DK states the following:

"The problem of illusion lies in the fact that it is a soul activity, and the result of the mind aspect of all the souls in manifestation. It is the soul which is submerged in the illusion, and the soul that fails to see with clarity until such time as it has learned to pour the light of the soul through into the mind and the brain."

This might be a revelation to you. You might never have thought that the soul could be restricted in any way. You might have thought that the restriction is always on the matter aspect, the personality, the inadequacy of the apparatus, physical, astral or mental, to allow the soul correct awareness of the outer world in which we live.

We provide the access for the soul, and if we do not have the apparatus, the soul cannot see. Most emphasis in the teaching has been that the apparatus is inadequate, and so it is. The inertia of matter itself makes it difficult, at times impossible, for the soul to use adequately the apparatus which is provided in a given incarnation by the personality. The result on the mental level is what we call illusion. The mind and brain misinterpret reality and what the soul sees. It is precisely the misinterpretation of reality that causes illusion.

We see the world, we take into our mind all the ideas, thoughtforms, ideologies and points of view, and try to make some sense out of them. We attach ourselves to these ideas and ideologies if they are attractive to us. We join this or that group or organization and in this way fill our minds with illusion.

We make it impossible for the soul to see clearly, truthfully, without hindrance, what the world is really like. We show the soul what we think the world is like. After we have traded with all the ideas, ideologies, political parties, ways of living and thinking, the different religions, doctrines and dogmas, we are left with a fog, lack of light, which we call illusion, thereby closing the mind of the personality to the light of the soul.

The soul seeks to pour its light through the mental body. When the illusion is on the astral level, we call it glamour. The world is filled with glamour. Some of you know some of your own glamours. Everyone in incarnation, except the Masters and the higher initiates, suffer from glamour or illusion. We do not see the world as it truly is. We live in the Great Illusion.

Most people who begin to think (this is the difference between glamour and illusion) use their thoughts and interpretations as if they were real, and choose among them. They like the feeling of something because they are sentimental, for example, and find a more sentimental way of expressing themselves. If they are a harder type of person they may find a harder approach is more to their taste. We attach ourselves to that which we can interpret, which we think is true.

"Illusion is primarily of a mental quality, and is characteristic of the attitude of mind of those people who are more intellectual than emotional. They have outgrown glamours as usually understood. It is the misunderstanding of

ideas and thoughtforms of which they are guilty, and of misinterpretations. . . .

"Today illusion is so potent, that few people whose minds are in any way developed but are controlled by these vast illusionary thoughtforms, which have their roots and draw their life from the lower personality life and desire nature of the masses of men."

We are living in a world that is beset with illusion. Every country in the world has its own illusions. If it is a large country like Russia or America, the people usually have illusions of grandeur. They seek to dominate, to enlarge. The larger you are, the more you seek to enlarge. It is an odd thing. You would think a country the size of Russia or the US would be so big that they would be tired of being so big. It would feel unwieldy and unco-ordinated. But no, they would like to be bigger.

You would think that having this great area called the United States, 3,000 miles across and a couple of thousand miles north to south, that would be enough to satisfy most people. But no. Where did Texas come from, New Mexico, half of California? The US stole them from Mexico. This desire to be the biggest and best, to aggrandize, to create this thoughtform of superiority, is a great existing illusion of the people of the United States. Today, under the present Republican administration, the US seems bent on the creation of a worldwide political and economic system dominated by America.

The British ruled a huge part of the world for nearly 200 years until the middle of the 20th century. Wherever you looked on the map of the world you saw pink. Where you saw pink that was Britain, British dominion and British colonies, all owned and ruled by Britain, well or badly. That gave Britain the great illusion that it was a megapower. For a short time it was a megapower.

When the Spaniards came and conquered most of South America, they took all the gold and silver they could find, and Spain became the richest country in the world. In Europe they felt powerful and dominant, but only for a time. This happens again and again.

The entry of Napoleon onto the world scene in Europe started the process whereby 'the glory that was France' became a powerful illusion, a powerful thoughtform. The French aspiration to change the corruption, the overblown civilization of the Louis Kings, became a military campaign of conquest led by Napoleon, which covered the whole of Europe and parts of Russia and Africa. This is the illusion of grandeur. The colonization which took place during the 16th, 17th, 18th and 19th centuries was all the result of the illusion of aggrandizement.

Today the United States is engaged in something similar, a programme of aggrandizement under the banner of a 'war against terrorism' and the creation of a Pax Americana around the world. The 2,000-plus foreign bases that the United States now has provide the necessary military access to 'police the world', as they would say. To be the policeman for the world, as the British saw themselves and now the Americans see themselves, is a huge illusion. It is untenable, ridiculous, and today is very disturbing to the peace of the world. That is illusion on a major scale.

Illusion goes all the way from the level of nations and world politics, to the illusions governing the working of groups like ourselves. Some groups have not gone out of incarnation, so to say, but have lost impact in the world, lost authority and reality because of the illusion of their original genesis.

I was thinking, for instance, of the Theosophical Society, which still does good work, publishes the Theosophical teachings, which gradually, quietly, spread the teachings of the Masters through H.P. Blavatsky and other writers. The vast majority of the early Theosophists saw themselves as the 'hard edge' of knowledge, the cutting edge of change of consciousness in the world. In a very real sense that was true because for the first time in living memory the ideas of Hierarchy became public. They took a public existence and were debated, put down, thought to be the work of the devil, just like any change in direction among adherents to any religion. Any change is seen as the 'work of the devil'.

Change can be good or bad, but if things are working you do not usually change them. When things are not working well, when the need for change, the need for new ideas, a new input of energy is apparent, it is a sure sign that the teaching of the time has reached a limit. It can no longer reveal anything, but is becoming more and more crystallized. The teaching of much of the world had reached just such a point when *The Secret Doctrine*, for instance, H.P. Blavatsky's major opus, was published.

Certainly in the religious field the door was tightly closed against this intrusion of Theosophy. Theosophy is the philosophy of God. You cannot get a bigger threat to religion than that, many thought, and yet Theosophy has never been against religion – on the contrary. The religionists of the time took exception to everything that was put forward by Madame Blavatsky. So, too, did the scientists of the time. The best known scientists were among her most stern critics, and even to this day whenever any mention is made of Madame Blavatsky in journals or the media she usually gets a very sour press indeed.

This is a woman who was a fourth-degree initiate, at the same level as Jesus in Palestine or Leonardo da Vinci, and yet she is still reviled as a fraud, a medium, who cheated in mediumistic séances (which she never did, did not need to) and so has had a terrible reputation thrust upon her.

This is really because the ideas stemming from Hierarchy are absolutely explosive. They upset the ideas of the time, which were ideas of illusion. The ideas given through Blavatsky, the ideas of Hierarchy, were deliberately sent into the world to clear the way, to get rid of the glamours and illusions which to this day bedevil the feeling and thinking of most people. The more intellectual the person, the more illusion will be their problem.

I was criticized recently for calling some so-called scientists "stupid" in *Share International*, in reference to their reaction to crop circles. As I was reading the Master DK the other day, I found a case in which He called certain scientists stupid. So I am in good company. He also says that all disciples must have courage, first and foremost. The world will never get rid of illusion until we have courage. One of the duties of true disciples, says DK, is to speak out openly against whatever authority exists in the world – scientific, religious, political or any level – with which we disagree and see further and clearer than it does.

If he thinks that they are wrong, it behoves a disciple to say so. If he just skulks and pretends that he has no point of view on the subject, and nothing better, clearer, more true to give, then he is a disciple only in name. The true disciple is the disciple who knows no fear. That is the number one essential for all disciples.

Recognizing Glamour and Illusion

According to DK, the only way that the problem of glamour can be overcome is through the mental body, by the soul through the mental body revealing the glamour. And He says: *"It is much that you have recognized that glamour and illusion exist. The majority of people are unaware of their presence."* You only have to talk to most people, and you will find that it is true. Most people are totally unaware that they are living in glamour and illusion.

"Many good people today see this not; they deify their glamours. . . ." They deify them! They think they are wonderful. *"The best thing I have is this glamour,"* whatever it happens to be, *". . . and regard their illusions as their prized and hard won possessions."*

People join political parties and organizations. Or they join a group which is not an organization and turn it into an organization with themselves in a position of power. It gives them the illusion of grandeur, importance. It is a hidden way to control. That is a major illusion which dominates all society.

All political parties, all so-called spiritual groups, all groups everywhere, gravitate to a situation in which they can control. The group as a whole might not, but individuals in the group do. That control gives them the feeling of power. It is the power they want, not the service that they think they are giving of a political, spiritual or religious nature. Consciously or unconsciously, they are after power. That is the big glamour and the huge illusion of their lives.

They may waste years struggling to get into a position, and to retain a position, against others in their particular group, whether religious, political, social, scientific or academic. Every institution you could name, every group that you could mention, has this problem besetting it today.

The Master DK says: *"Today illusion is so potent, that few people whose minds are in any way developed, but are controlled by these vast illusionary thoughtforms, which have their roots and draw their life from the lower personality life and desire nature of the masses of men. . . .*

"Illusion is the mode whereby limited understanding and material knowledge interpret truth, veiling and hiding it behind a cloud of thoughtforms. Those thoughtforms become

then more real than the truth they veil, and consequently control man's approach to Reality."

There are many problems in the world, but the problem of consciousness is precisely that the more educated you are, the more advanced you are in your profession, the more in illusion you are likely to be because it provides the format for this desire to control. The institution, whether religious, political or academic, provides a structure whereby a man or woman can advance higher and higher into a position of more and more power and control.

They are advancing in their profession in a position of power, in the ability to control events, money, people, in their institution. That is the major glamour which besets everything from the Pentagon to the stock exchanges of the world. It is the same glamour, the same illusion that this is meaningful. The idea that making money makes for happiness, or making more money makes for greater happiness, is a thoughtform. If you are living in desperate circumstances, barely able to eat, to clothe and educate your children, then obviously earning more money would alleviate that stress. But the idea that you need to become a millionaire, and becoming a millionaire that you need to become a billionaire, and that the way to do it is to invest in the stock exchange, is an illusion.

People are involved daily, hourly, reading the trade papers on how to make money, how to get more money out of the money that they have invested. It is living off the world, giving nothing back. It is simply gambling, investing money, making it double, treble, many times. Making a fortune on the stock exchange adds nothing to society. It is one huge, illusionary thoughtform and millions of people in every country have accepted that as a reality.

That is why Maitreya calls the stock exchanges "the gambling casinos of the world". They owe nothing to society; they give nothing to society. They allow some people with money to spare to make more without doing anything at all, not working for it, but simply making money available, the interest on which is giving you an easy life.

These thoughtforms cloud and fill our lives. They are not a passing fancy. Everything I have said about illusion is going on now and constitutes the life of most people, most of the time.

Also, and this is perhaps more sinister: *"This form of illusion is becoming increasingly prevalent among disciples, and those who have taken the first two initiations. . . . The significance of their attainment pours in upon them, and the sense of their responsibility and their knowledge. Again they over-estimate themselves, regarding their missions and themselves as unique among the sons of men, and their esoteric and subjective demand for recognition enters in and spoils what might otherwise have been a fruitful service. Any emphasis upon the personality can distort most easily the pure light of the soul, as it seeks to pour through the lower self. Any effort to call attention to the mission or task which the personality has undertaken detracts from that mission, and handicaps the man in his task; it leads to the deferring of its fulfilment until such time when the disciple can be naught but a channel through which love can pour, and light can shine. This pouring through and shining forth has to be a spontaneous happening, and contain no self-reference."*

How often do we see or hear of groups led by some individual which for a little time, a season, a year or two, come to some prominence? One sees it, or used to see it very much, here in the US. Every time I came to the US from 1980 onwards I would hear of and occasionally meet some well known 'guru' or teacher who had a large group. They would be living in a gifted retreat in the country, in the mountains, in beautiful, wonderful places.

If I met the person, I usually found them glamoured to a degree that was literally painful. I would try not to show it, of course, and we never seemed to get further than that. Six months or a year later you would not hear anything more about that group, or only that they had got into difficulties and had squandered $400,000 on the buildings, which were being taken back by the benefactor. There was always some monkey-business, usually to do with money.

This happened because the essence of the group was not real. It was based on a fantasy. Probably the individual who started the group had a sense of service, or had an 'experience'. Perhaps he was astrally sensitive, in touch with some entity, perhaps on the fifth or sixth astral plane, and was receiving quite nice, well-formed thoughts and ideas on that level. They would attract the type of person who could respond to that level. But there would not be those who would demand more clarity, more contact with the outside world, the world of reality, and so the group would fold of its own volition, and you would hear no more about it. That happens over and over again.

On the more dramatic side, you might find that they had all killed themselves, had taken poison or shot each other. All sorts of horrible stories decorate the history of some of the quainter 'spiritual' groups. But that 'spiritual' is 99 per cent of the time based on a huge illusion – the illusion of the founder and those who followed the founder into the fire, into death, into the mountains or wherever.

My daughter recently met Maitreya in Hyde Park in London. She was in a hurry on some errand, and an elderly gentleman joined her and they started walking along together. He said: "I am going to tell you something very important." She was all ears, of course. He said: "Everything is energy. Everything is made up of energy, vibrating in little molecules. And everything made of energy has its opposite.

For instance, you may be depressed this year, fed up, things not going well, and who is to say that next year it will not all be different? It could all be pleasant and happy-making. Everything is like that. It is all changing, changing. For instance, look at Mr Blair. He has built himself up and up and up." And the man said: "Look at him. He is bound to come tumbling, tumbling, down." He said this and claimed a kiss on the cheek as her payment for the information. They parted and went on their way.

This shows how, from the point of view of Hierarchy looking at the world, They see the glamours, They see reality. They see and know that what we see is entirely different from the truth. The truth cannot be seen by the soul because the personality does not allow the soul to see the truth. We have hidden the truth.

We see the idea. Out of our false language, false education, our ignorance, lack of understanding, we interpret according to the 'norm', the academic line, the accepted understanding, whether that is political, religious or academic.

We accept the status quo, in other words. That is because we are afraid to make changes. We are afraid to change so we do not see the need for change. We cover the need for change, the reality which is there, the true state of the world, the pain, the suffering, the insecurity of the world. I do not mean only terrorism, but the insecurity of life, including, of course today, terrorism, because we do not want to see it. It is too upsetting, too frightening, and so we cover it over with illusion. We fill every fragment of life with illusion.

We do it as groups, in political parties, as governments. They all have their different ways of functioning with this trick of covering up the truth. What is the answer? How can we get out of it?

Intuition

The Master DK says only the intuition can overcome illusion.

"It is in meditation and in the technique of mind control, that the thinkers of the world will begin to rid the world of illusion. Hence the increasing interest in meditation as the weight of the world glamour is increasingly realized, and hence the vital necessity for right understanding of the way of mind control. . . . Only the intuition can dispel illusion, and hence the need for training intuitives."

The intuition is the light of the soul, the buddhic level of the soul working directly through the mind. When the mind is cleared of illusion, the buddhi or intuition itself can manifest. When intuition or buddhi manifests, it automatically clears the mind of the individual from all these illusions. It is like cleaning house. One day you go into a house and see the cobwebs. You have been in that house every day for years and you never saw that the place is covered with cobwebs. One day when you notice the cobwebs you take a brush and start to clear them.

The faculty we call intuition is the next level of the mind to be developed. Most people at the present level of humanity are working with ratiocination, thinking. We can think. The more we can think, the cleverer we think we are.

Unfortunately, people in esoteric groups think that they are clearer in the esoteric sense because they are in an esoteric group. But they could be even more glamoured, and often are, than their colleagues who do not know anything about esotericism. The esoteric groups are among the most glamoured and illusion-ridden of any groups in the world.

If someone is in a position of authority or some degree of attainment in the outer world, and is also in an esoteric group, they tend to put the two together and think that in the esoteric group they should have the control, the power, which they would have in the academic, religious or scientific field. In an esoteric group it does not work. There is no position of power in a truly esoteric group.

This is the big issue I have spoken about before, the problem of organization versus an organic form of organization. There are those who enter a group like this, for instance, and organize, organize, organize. They think they are good at organizing. Perhaps they are and perhaps they are not, but it is has nothing to do with the esoteric nature of the group.

An esoteric group does not function through organization. In fact, DK says that the Theosophical Society foundered on the "rock of organization". Once H.P. Blavatsky died and left the field, the main work collapsed because her soul was not involved in the group. She was a fourth-degree initiate. She worked only through her soul-infused personality, and when the personality went, because she died, the group foundered.

It foundered on the rock of the organization that the 'clever' people had brought in. HPB was not a clever person. She was an absolute genius, one of the world's great initiates. But not a 'smart alec' like some of the people who came in and built up the structure of the Theosophical Society, spread it throughout the world, and created the block to the essence of the Theosophical teachings that has prevented it from making much headway since the days of Annie Besant. According to the Master DK they crystallized the teachings and closed the minds of the society to the democratic ideas of Alice Bailey, and to the new teaching which was given through Alice Bailey by that Master.

You have to be very clear. Everyone in this group has to look at themselves and try to discover where they are glamoured and where they are filled with illusion. What they think are their best qualities, the best qualities they bring to bear in the group, are probably their greatest illusions. It is almost a truism to say that. That is why DK says "their most prized possessions". What they have worked hard for and developed in their lives, when it comes to reality, to being a disciple, have little value.

We present our experiences through our misinterpretations, which are all bound up with the personality, the self. They make the self feel secure. They may relate to the idea of patriotism: "I am American," or "I am British," or "I am French, therefore I am great." These are thoughtforms which condition the life of nations. Almost every Briton is a patriot. They all think that British footballers are the best in the world, which is a nonsense. Nobody else thinks that British football is the best in the world. It used to be the best – but not for a long time. Look at the flags all over America. I have never seen a country so decorated with flags.

Clear thinking

"The objective of all training given on the Path of Discipleship, and up to the third initiation, is to induce that clear thinking which will render the disciple free from illusion. . . ."

It is to do with the freedom of our thinking. It has to be clear. We are so full of glamour that even when we become educated and begin to use our mental faculties to quite an extent, it is still full of glamour, or as we call it, illusion, on the mental plane. It is so difficult to look at life as it really is because we do not clear the path for the soul to show us life as it is. The soul looks out, and it sees what we have presented to it as reality. And so the soul is lost in the illusion. That is a major problem for the world.

". . . to induce that clear thinking which will render the disciple free from illusion, and give to him that emotional stability and poise which gives no room for the entrance of any of the world glamour. . . .

"One of the problems which confronts the aspirant is the problem of duly recognizing glamour when it arises, and of being aware of the glamours which beset his path and the illusions which build a wall between him and the light. It is much that you have recognized that glamour and illusion exist."

We all know that glamour and illusion exist. Do you know that as an esoteric statement, or do you know that as a result of experience? How much do you recognize that glamour and illusion exist? Can you see it in yourself? Can you deal with it on a day-to-day basis? Or is it just an idea you have taken from reading the Master DK and say: "Yes, I accept that glamour is a terrible thing, and illusion, yes, that is terrible." You accept that they exist. Or do you see that they exist? You have to see it. You have to experience, see, where it is hiding the truth, where people are hiding the truth, when they are not true. They think they are true. They mean to be true. They all mean well. Most people in a group like this, for instance, mean well, but the action is often different from the meaning.

The Master DK says: *"The world of phenomena is not denied, but we regard the mind as misinterpreting it, and as refusing to see it as it is in reality. We consider this misinterpretation as constituting the Great Illusion. . . .*

"An aspirant succeeds in contacting his soul or ego through right effort. Through meditation, good intention and correct technique, plus the desire to serve and to love, he achieves alignment. He becomes then aware of the results of his successful work. His mind is illumined. A sense of power flows through his vehicles. He is, temporarily at least, made aware of the Plan. The need of the world and the capacity of the soul to meet that need flood his consciousness. His dedication, consecration and right purpose enhance the directed inflow of spiritual energy. He knows. He loves. He seeks to serve, and does all three more or less successfully.

The result of all this is that he becomes more engrossed with the sense of power, and with the part he is to play in aiding humanity, than he is with the realization of a due and proper sense of proportion and of spiritual values. He over-estimates his experience and himself. Instead of redoubling his efforts, and thus establishing a closer contact with the kingdom of souls [the Masters], and loving all beings more deeply, he begins to call attention to himself, to the mission he is to develop, and to the confidence that the Master and even the planetary Logos apparently have in him. He talks about himself; he gestures and attracts notice, demanding recognition. As he does so, his alignment is steadily impaired; his contact lessens, and he joins the ranks of the many who have succumbed to the illusion of sensed power. This form of illusion is becoming increasingly prevalent among disciples, and those who have taken the first two initiations."

How to Get Rid of Glamour

How can you get rid of this terrible reality of glamour and illusion? Glamour is, at a lower level, the sum total of all the emotional reactions, and thoughtforms created by them, of the masses of people from the beginning of time. It is endless and deep and squalid and unbearable. To a Master, because He has a clear view, it must seem an endless struggle to rid humanity of this terrible weight.

Any effort to free humanity of the weight, the confines of glamour, must be a tremendous day for Hierarchy. This is achieved through experience, through learning to look at the glamours, recognizing them, and working seriously at overcoming them.

We can always recognize glamours in other people; that is the easiest thing in the world. Everybody else has glamours. The difficulty is to see our own. To see our own glamours, this is the thing. To see them and measure them, to see the ones which are deep and important, like fear, the worst of all the glamours, the one from which probably all the worst glamours come. To see that fear is the root of all unhappiness, all suffering in the world, and to try to recognize the illusions. That means using the faculty of intuition.

It is difficult to do this because you have to have intuition before you can use it. But we all have it in potential, and intuition is that faculty of the mind which will supersede the faculty which most people think so highly of today, their ability to think, to rationalize. Ratiocination has become the way we can make 'miracles'. We can make bombs that will kill people, hundreds of thousands at a time. We can make rockets that will go to the moon and back.

We are pretty good at designing, not always correctly, because all sorts of illusions and glamours come into the process. The Americans are good at some things and the Russians are better at other things, because the illusions of the particular country colour what they do. The illusions colour their ability to carry out a task, depending on how much importance they give to it, and how much or how little money they are prepared to spend.

For example, the Russians have achieved a kind of mastery of space as far as this planet is concerned, on a relatively small output of money. The Americans have achieved more spectacular things. They have sent a man to the moon. The Americans have much more sophisticated instruments in some ways, but they are so sophisticated that they go wrong. There have been some tragic results in sending groups of people into space for one reason or another. There have been two relatively recently. Some of these were expected, even predicted, by workers at NASA, who were at a lesser level than the operatives who had the final say, and therefore not taken account of. These men warned about a piston ring or covering, for example. They warned that they were done in such a way that they might go wrong, that they would leak, and in fact that is what caused one of the most tragic accidents. The warnings were given but nothing was done about them because they came from a man who had no particular authority. He was a worker on the project but the glamour of authority, the glamour of a person in authority knowing better than a person not in authority, took over, and his warnings went unattended.

Likewise, when the Masters warned the US military, three months before 9/11, about the likelihood of a terrorist attack in September 2001, nothing was done about it. They warned them about the Pentagon and the White House. They did not say anything about the Twin Towers, but They warned them that an event of real importance involving the Pentagon and probably the White House would take place. You would have thought that something would have been done. But so great is the illusion that America is impregnable, so great is that thoughtform in the mind of the people who run the country from the Pentagon, that nothing was done. America is run more from the Pentagon than from the White House, although they both have different functions. The Pentagon has the last say about what is done or not done. They ignored what was told them and the result was tragic, the 9/11 catastrophe.

That is the result of both glamour and illusion. The glamour is that "we can do anything we like. We are so strong, so rich, so powerful", even if it is not the case. Japan owns 31 per cent of the national debt of America. If Japan and one or two other countries, or even if Japan alone, withdrew their money, cashed the American bonds which it has invested in, which support the US national debt, America would collapse. The stock market would go down and down. It would be a catastrophe for America. That is all it would take.

With all that illusion and glamour, therefore, they did not expect that 9/11 could happen to America. It did, and it will again if the security powers in this country do not take seriously any future warnings. They might be lucky. They might forestall it. They may have already forestalled such events. It is essential that people see the world clearly as it is, not as they want it to be.

America in the aftermath of 9/11 had the sympathy of the whole world. Everybody loved America, felt for America. Everyone said: "That could have been anywhere, in any developed country in the world." Now the opposite is the case. America is reviled, hated and feared. It is reviled and hated because it is feared. And it is feared because it is distrusted. Nobody trusts the present US administration not to upset the balance of the world, which is what they are trying to do. That is a huge illusion, but an illusion that could be true. Illusions may be false, but they can be about real situations. The illusion that America is powerful and ready for anything might be the very factor that makes it possible to pull off a 9/11.

It does no good for anyone to live in illusion. It may feel more comfortable, but essentially it cuts you off from reality. Develop the intuition. The way to develop the intuition is to meditate, do Transmission Meditation, the number one meditation to bring about soul development and intuition. Divinity is that blessed state in which you see reality absolutely clearly. That cannot be done with only the faculties of the lower mind. It is not possible to see reality with the physical, astral and mental body alone.

At most, we can be head of the government, the bank, of the institution. We can be at the top of our profession, but it does not mean much at all in terms of point in evolution. Extraordinary work is done by people whose minds are somewhat evolved and used, and yet these same people might well not have taken the first initiation. In fact, they might take the first initiation sooner if they were not the head of the bank, or the headmaster of the college.

Evolution is to do with beingness, with the extent of the soul infusion at any given time. If the soul is immersed in its vehicle, and sees reality through it, then it may be evolved. But if it is only able to think, to use the brain, it is using the faculties of the lower mind. That is no way of measuring the point reached in evolution. One of the big glamours and illusions of people in the so-called esoteric groups is that they believe, because they are in an esoteric group, that they are rather evolved. Very often they are not as evolved as people who have never heard of esotericism or the Master DK or any such thing. One has to be very honest with oneself to be a disciple.

[Note: The quotations from Alice A. Bailey are all taken from the section on 'Illusion' in *Ponder On This*, the compilation by Aart Jurriaanse.]

ILLUSION

QUESTIONS AND ANSWERS

Edited version of the Question and Answer session with Benjamin Creme from the 2003 Transmission Meditation Conferences held in San Francisco, USA, and Kerkrade, the Netherlands.

SOUL, PERSONALITY, INTUITION

It was a surprise to hear that the soul cannot always recognize the truth because it is tainted by the personality. Many of us in our group were under the illusion that the soul was all-knowing. Can you elaborate on this?

There is a misunderstanding here. The soul is all-knowing. The soul is not 'tainted' by the personality. The soul is not reduced one iota in its Being by its inability to manifest through the vehicles of the personality, in this case the mental body.

The vehicles of the personality misinterpret what the soul sees and present that to the soul. Because of the illusions, the mental body does not see reality; it does not see the truth. So it presents that to the soul, and the soul works through the mental body. The mental body presents these illusions as if they were reality and truth.

If the soul has not reached the point where it can manifest its light unencumbered through the mental body, unaffected by the illusions of the personality, this can induce a state of miscalculation for the soul because it is presented with wrong data. The soul cannot see the truth because the truth is not presented to it by the mental body.

A construction, an idea, an ideology, a series of thoughtforms, are presented to the soul moment-to-moment as the reality which the soul is seeing through the mental body. It may be wrong but it does not affect the soul on its own plane. The soul remains perfect, inviolable. It is simply inadequate to function at this level if the vehicle does not allow it, if the vehicles of the personality present distorted thoughtforms about the nature of reality.

The soul depends on the vehicles. It provides itself with vehicles in order to see the reality at this level. Where these vehicles are inadequate, the view of the soul is distorted. That is what illusion is and does.

My understanding is that soul functions on the upper four sub-planes of the mental plane, and the personality functions on the lower three sub-planes of the mental plane.

The soul functions on the highest (4th) sub-plane of the mental planes. The illusions in the mind of the individual condition the ability of the soul to see reality. If the mind itself is not clear, if it presents an unclear picture of reality, the soul cannot see clearly. That is what illusion is, and the problem is that it is a soul problem.

A mind caught in illusion hinders the expression of the soul's light. The way to dispel illusion is through intuition, which is a soul quality. This seems to be a paradox. We need to use a soul quality to increase expression of the soul when we are immersed in illusion. Please elucidate.

You have to use a soul quality to get rid of the illusion which is preventing the expression of the soul light. That is a paradox. There are such things as paradoxes. You have to learn to like the paradox.

I have found that most people hate paradox. They think if this is true, then that cannot be true. If America is the best of all countries, if the market forces economy is the best of all possible economies in the world, then it cannot be true that there is any good in communism. I personally think there is good in communism. Compare the Russian with the American Constitution; they are very similar in their ideals.

The trouble with communism is that it came from above. It was imposed by about 10 million people, at the most on 250 million people. They had to accept it whether they liked it or not. It did not grow out of the people but was imposed from above by the party. It was very difficult to become a member of the party. Only about 10 million people actually became members. They ran the Soviet Union, which was vast, and covered one-sixth of the world's surface. What they left out was the need for freedom. Individual freedom is essential. But so is justice. In the US you have a degree of individual freedom but little justice. You need both justice and freedom. It is a paradox, but it is true. The best justice in the world is freedom. The best freedom in the world is justice.

Developed intuition overcomes the illusion. If you have intuition, you do not have illusion. It is not as if you go on having the illusion but you use intuition to get rid of it while you have it. You use intuition, the developed faculty of the soul, to clarify the view of life, which is what illusion is not doing. Illusion makes a fog between the observer and the world, and the result is fantasy, illusion. If the soul light, the intuition, is allowed to play, if that faculty is used, the illusion does not arise.

It is not that illusion is existing and cannot be ended. It is changed. You exchange illusion for intuition. Intuition when used sweeps the board clean. It is like a brush, getting rid of the cobwebs. All that prevents the experience of reality is clarified and swept aside, and you know. When you know from the intuition, there is no room for any illusion. It does not arise.

Telling the difference between intuition and wishful thinking can be difficult. Do you have any suggestions for distinguishing them?

Many people think 'wishfully'. People construct thoughtforms all the time. That wishful thinking very often includes a scenario in which the wish is fulfilled. It is like dreaming. They go to bed and say: "I am going to dream something nice tonight. I will dream I am on holiday, and it is lovely. It is in Hawaii, and the coconuts are falling from the trees." They elaborate on it, and then they go to bed and dream. That is wishful thinking.

How do you distinguish between that and direct intuition? The difference between intuition and wishful thinking shows in its ability to reveal. Wishful thinking fulfils a dream, a thoughtform, a longing, a desire. Whereas the intuition, if it is true intuition, always reveals something; it is revelatory. If it is not revelatory, then it is not intuition at all.

One thing intuition is not, is wishful thinking. To wish for something strongly, with an enormous love of the world, is not intuition. Intuition is the function of the soul looking into the world and giving its revelation, its ability to reveal outwardly to the world. It can only do that when there is no barrier of glamour, or in this case, illusion, to restrict its revelatory ability.

The soul unencumbered on its own plane can reveal. It knows love and revelation, and it knows without thinking. That is the essence of intuition. The soul does not have to think. It already knows. At the level where it can become potent in the life, it reveals itself as revelation. The person then begins to know without having to think and rationalize. The rationalizing mind can cope with the effects of the lower concrete life and mind of the personality. When the soul is functioning unrestrictedly, then intuition takes the place of rationalizing.

Eventually, as a race, ratiocination – the ability to rationalize, to work things out and come to a conclusion as a result – will drop below the level of consciousness and be replaced by intuition. This is the way forward for the race as a whole. This only occurs when a person is becoming imbued with the nature of the soul and is working on the personality to purify the vehicles of the soul, to enable that to take place.

The vehicles cause the problem. The vehicle of the mind throws up these illusions, these thoughtforms, ideas, belief patterns, all this wrong thinking, and so the soul is not able to work directly from the soul level and through intuition reveal what the person wants to know.

People with mental equipment along the 2-4-6 ray line are more likely to develop the intuition, at least earlier or more easily, than those along the 1-3-5-7 line. But whatever the ray structure, the disciple is not accepted as a disciple until the intuitive faculty is somewhat developed and demonstrating.

We are talking about people who are somewhat evolved as far as humanity as a whole is concerned. The more evolved the person is, the more the intuitive faculty functions, and the more that person does not need to rationalize. This is true for all disciples, whatever the ray structure.

There comes a time when the soul itself develops in two directions. It turns to the monad and receives the energy of the monad, but it also turns to its reflection, the man or woman in incarnation. It forms a certain profound unification, a union at a very deep level, between the monad and the personality. It is to do with the soul infusion of the vehicles. As a person's physical, astral and mental vehicles vibrate more and more at the same level, they become synchronized. There is a synthesis produced by the soul.

When the physical and astral bodies are sufficiently synthesized and the mental body is at least beginning to be synthesized, the demonstration of intuition begins automatically to take place. When the energy of the monad is brought in by the soul, intuition is registering as a normal faculty of the person. It may still to some degree be coloured by illusion.

Some advanced people have been so illusionary that they thought they were the Christ. I am talking about people like Bahá'u'lláh and Meher Baba. Bahá'u'lláh introduced the Bahai teachings, which were given by Maitreya. He was overshadowed by Maitreya, Who dictated the teachings to him. Bahá'u'lláh himself, who was a third-degree initiate, thought they came directly from God. He had this illusion, this thoughtform, that God existed up in the sky and dictated these teachings to him. He was receiving them from the Christ but he thought he was the Christ. That is illusion. That is a very powerful thoughtform, misinterpretation of reality at a very high level. It is not simple and automatic; people evolve unequally.

Meher Baba, for example, was a religious genius. He was 2.4 degrees initiate, but nevertheless he had certain fantasies, illusions, about his own personal life. Meher Baba, too, believed that he was the Christ. He became muni (stopped speaking) for about 20 years, and then he wrote: "When I start to speak again I will be the Christ." He died before he could be the Christ! You cannot be the Christ at 2.4. It is just not possible. That is a major glamour, or in this case, illusion.

What is the difference between glamour and illusion?

It is the same illusion – that is, an absence of clarity, of light, of revelation, of meaning. If your mind is closed or obscured from the truth, then you are living in illusion. If it is experienced as an emotion, then it is glamour; if it is a mental notion or idea, then it is illusion.

Glamour is illusion on the astral/emotional plane. Illusion is illusion on the mental plane. It involves the soul because the soul is using the mental plane which has to be clear. If it is not clear, the soul is not clear, it cannot look clearly out at the world. It sees the world through a mass of illusions, of which the person is unaware. The person thinks he is a smart guy. He has brilliant ideas. He is leading the group into a great new future. He is head of state, is developing the weapons to make his country the best and strongest in the world. He is becoming a great man.

People in all groups, though they probably do not know it, are filled with illusions: about themselves, their sincerity, their devotion to the cause. They have consecrated their life to service. Let them look clearly. If any aspect of their life is threatened, when there is any threat to their well-being, their 'comfort zone', then let us see where their consecration and devotion come in. When they look, they will see that often what they think they are doing is not what they are actually doing.

Everyone has illusions. They are not something that we can go through life and avoid. We have them, and we have to get rid of them, deal with them. The only way to deal with illusions is to develop the intuition. How do you do that? We learn to do it by controlling the mind, because it is the controlled mind that can avoid illusion. There are all sorts of techniques to control and develop the mind.

In the first place, I would suggest as a means of beginning to control the mind, employing the power of the mind, finding out where the mind really is. How much of the mind is at our disposal or how much of it is fragmented into the subconscious and feeding all these thoughtforms that produce the glamour and illusion?

There is a technique of self-hypnosis that you can develop. A book by a Canadian named Rolf Alexander called *The Power of the Mind* describes a technique of self-hypnosis, the gradual freeing of the mind from fragmentation in the subconscious. The subconscious mind should be subconscious. It should just go on unconsciously carrying out your digestion, feeding your blood and cells through the different parts of the body, a purely automatic process below the threshold of consciousness.

The emotions of the individual are the outcome of the misuse of the energy of the astral body. The astral body should be a still, calm lake, in which the energy we call buddhi, the second of the three soul aspects, can be reflected. When it is reflected, you have intuition. Soul insight reflected as buddhi provides the intuition. Where there is the usual turmoil of the astral body, which most people have, there is no tranquil lake on which the soul can reflect its buddhic consciousness.

The Power of the Mind is very interesting in that it provides a very simple process of self-hypnosis whereby you can free the mind from its fragmentation in the subconscious. Every time you go to sleep you dream. You dream whether you remember the dream or not, but dreams are just the result of the thought-forming faculty of the human mind. The process is such that the mind, which is not accessible in sleep, becomes accessible in the form of dreams. The thought-forming process goes on, and you have the most wonderful, creative dreams.

Dreams are like films. You can create anything in them. You just think of it, and it is there in your dream instantly. On the mental plane the same activity is going on only at a higher turn of the spiral, involving ideas and concepts rather than desires. It inhibits the ability of the soul to see reality.

In *The Power of the Mind*, first of all, you send yourself to sleep. You give yourself certain affirmations. You give yourself a certain time to wake up. You wake up and gradually develop what are in the affirmations. Your mind, from being fragmented in the subconscious, is gradually lifted up. Your body remains asleep, but your mind is lifted out of that sleeping body which is locked, you cannot move it. Anyone can do it; it is very simple. Your mind comes up and up and out, and then you are clear. It is a completely different experience of mind from the mind absorbed in the subconscious, which is the normal condition.

The degree to which your mind is submerged in the unconscious is the degree to which you are limited in mind. When your mind is partly submerged, you do not have the full energy of the mental plane. The more your mind is absorbed and fragmented, to that degree it is unavailable to you as a person. As soon as you begin to free your mind from this fragmenting process, you free the energy of the mind, and your mind grows in relation to it. Being free, it is free also of illusion, and that allows intuition to come into play.

At our level (of point in evolution)* does the distinction between illusion and glamour really come into play?
It does, otherwise I would not have given this talk on illusion. It is important for disciples, probationers or aspirants to discipleship to awaken to the nature of glamour, the nature of illusion, and how this restricts the faculty of the soul in its process of revelation. It is very much to the benefit of the groups to address it.
[* Referring to the people who are mostly astrally polarized in their consciousness, somewhere between 0.8-1.5 in evolution.]

What kind of mind-control techniques will help us to develop more intuition and to use the rational mind less?
You do not want to use the rational mind less. What will happen is that the rationalization faculty will drop below the

level of consciousness. That does not mean we stop using the rational mind.

You use the faculties that you have. If you have a rationalizing mind then you use it. But you do not use it when it does not work. It does not work on the higher level, only on the lower mental planes.

The ignorant scientists of the world think that the rational mind does everything. They think they can find the answer to every problem, that all knowledge that it is possible to find can be found by their lower rational mind. They are wrong, their minds are closed. They do not even read books like those by the Master DK, which will teach them more about the faculty of the mind than anything in all the books of their own science. Being closed, they are ignorant and also extremely arrogant. So much so that they can say that a 'milk miracle' is caused by capillary action: that the milk somehow drips down the tiny lines of the bronze, copper or brass statues and the structure somehow absorbs the milk and makes it disappear. They can assert that, but it is illogical and unscientific.

They also refuse to open their minds to the masses of information about UFOs and crop circles. They refuse to address the evidence which is piling up all over the world, because they do not know the answers and are afraid to say "I do not know".

It is the same with every so-called miracle. A miracle is only a miracle if you do not know the science. Because of the restrictions of the lower mind, and because of the scientists' ignorance and arrogance, which has led them to make certain laws in the world (everything has to behave within these laws whether they are laws of the Earth or not), they do not see (because they refuse to see) that we are in the midst of the most extraordinary manifestation of the relationship between the planets that we have ever had on this planet.

They close their minds to it deliberately because they are afraid to demonstrate their ignorance. They are supported by all these quasi-scientists who go along with this attitude, acclaim it, and think that it is science. 'Science rules' – but science knows almost nothing. Modern science knows a tiny fraction of the nature of the universe or even of planet Earth, or of the laws which govern the manifestation of a planet or a solar system. The sooner they come down from the pedestal on which they have been placed, the sooner they will find the answers to some of their problems. These are mainly psychological!

If meditation and mind control develop the intuition, please elaborate on the way to induce mind control.

I have mentioned ways and means: meditation, self-hypnosis. There are many methods. The Masters, in Their training schools, teach mind control. It is one of the things, especially as a person is coming up to the third initiation. They teach mind control and the capacity to deal with illusion. Usually, by the time a person is working for the third initiation, it is taken for granted that he or she will have, to all intents and purposes, mastered glamour. They will not suffer from glamour to any great extent.

In my experience, however, glamour goes on and on. I think only a Master is entirely free from glamour. But it would not be called glamour. It would be called illusion, probably. Illusion on the mental plane involves the soul, so it is specific and needs special care and treatment.

People receive teaching and training, and nobody mentions this. The process of teaching has changed in Hierarchy because of the transformation of modern life and modern communications. It is open house all day, more or less. More people have jobs now right through the night than ever before in the history of the world. And more people, if they do not have jobs, stay up working in some way, or talking.

Artificial light has brought the facility of late-night work, and the mechanics of our modern society has induced 24-hour work around the clock. So Hierarchy have adapted, and if you are working at night, you can train during the day. Whenever you are asleep you can be trained.

Is moving beyond thought part of the key to mind control and ending illusions? If so, does moving beyond the process of thought elicit the light of the soul into the mind and thus develop the intuition?

Yes. The moving beyond the process of thought is a meditation. Meditation is one of the ways of 'controlling' the mind, not by controlling it, refusing the mind the possibility to think, that is inhibiting, simply strangling, the mind in its process of thinking. To go beyond thought is not to strangle thought.

To go beyond thought is literally to go beyond thought. That is a process of meditation, much used in the East by Masters and Avatars. It is a process of 'plunging in', as they call it. You find the source of the self, the 'I' thought, which you find to be at the heart centre, the seat of the soul in the etheric physical body. Being aware of the 'I' thought, you go beyond that. You plunge inward on the 'I' thought.

In the process you can think: "Who am I? Who am I?" You find you point to the heart centre as the source of 'I'. To find the 'I' you have to locate the 'I' thought. You find that the thought of 'I' and the breath come from one and the same source. When you slow down the breathing, you slow down the process of thought. When it is slowed down until it is barely functioning at all, you can plunge into the heart centre, into the soul. That is going beyond thought, but that is a state of meditation.

In that state of meditation no illusions appear. In meditating in this way you free yourself, to a great degree, from establishing future illusions. While you are doing it you cannot think, because you have gone beyond thought. It is a process of meditation rather than a process of thinking.

To think correctly is to think without illusion, which is not the same as meditation. To meditate correctly, you free your mind of illusion, because meditation clears the mind.

Is Transmission Meditation more beneficial for dissipating personal and world glamour than the techniques previously given by the Master DK in **Glamour: A World Problem?**

More beneficial because it is more effective. It is for people who are ready and able to serve, but they are probably at the same time expected to be putting into practice in their personal lives the techniques previously given by DK in *Glamour: A World Problem*. Glamour is glamour whatever you do. If you do Transmission Meditation, glamour will gradually fall away. It is not either/or, but together.

What is the meaning of the statement "we have to look at glamours without illusion"?

Most people have both glamours and illusions. Illusions deal with ideas, with mental thoughtforms. Everybody has them. The world's mental body, the mental plane, is filled with billions of thoughtforms – huge, small, ever-growing, always changing. These are mental thoughtforms.

There are also astral/emotional thoughtforms; they involve rather the action of the emotions. With emotional thoughtforms we experience a feeling, a sensation, and we put a meaning on it. That meaning, if it is not true, is glamour. You can only know it is glamour by the action of the mental body on it. Glamour is overcome by the light of the soul playing on the glamour through the mental body. The insight of the mental body has to be used to overcome the glamour. The light of the soul, which is the intuition, has to be used to overcome the mental thoughtforms which are illusions. They are either illusionary or they are true. The truth is always there, you do not have to discover it. If you have no glamour, you do not experience glamorous feelings; your feelings are true. They are coming from the heart, not the solar plexus; they are not a misuse of astral energy. If the ideas are true, they are coming from the soul and are creative, revelatory, illuminating. If they are illusory, they are false. It takes the intuition, the light of the soul, to show the falsity of it.

How do you recognize if your intuition is pure and not coloured by illusion and glamour?

By seeing if it works. When the intuition is functioning you know because you know because you know. You have not thought about it – you just know that it is. How do you know that it is intuition and not illusion? By experience. Because it works. Because it illumines. Because it conforms to the teachings given for thousands of years and is not a fantasy.

The next phase of humanity's development is indeed the development of intuition. The people of Europe and America, in particular, are the fifth sub-race of the fifth root race, using the 5th ray [of Concrete Mind] as their particular vehicle of expression. This has led to the huge explosion of science in the world over the last 120-130 years. It is the result of that ray being poured into the world in tremendous potency. It has good and bad results. It has opened the mind of people to the realities of the physical world. It has got rid of thousands of superstitions, and has created its own kind of superstitions as well. It has closed the minds of millions of people (particularly the wise scientists themselves) to the deeper nature of reality, but, on the other hand, it has led to the development of radio, television, telephones, faxes, emails.

That is the way the 5th-ray stimulus has activated our capacity to invent, to discover the nature of electricity, or at least begin to, and the spread of information through the electronic field and so on. There is a huge illusion connected with it because it leaves out, necessarily, a vast area of experience which has nothing to do with this concrete physical world. It limits the experience of humanity to the dense-physical plane. That is why it is so difficult to get certain ideas across today. It has taken years and years to tell the world about the reappearance of the Christ. You should be able to do that in a couple of years. Because of the fracturing of reality into just the physical plane there is a great, incredulous scepticism hanging over us, created by the 5th ray of lower mind. It is right on its own level, of course. The fault, the illusion, is that the scientists mistake the level that they see on as being the totality. Of course, it is not. It is only one level.

They look at a wood and they do not see it as a wood but as so many trees; they count the trees. They know it is a wood because they have counted the trees. Having counted them they accept that it is a wood. But they only see the trees.

The next sub-race of the 5th root race will see the development of the intuition on a massive scale. So how do you recognize that it is indeed intuition? It is a question of experience, you recognize it through detached experience. When you have gone through this struggle with glamour and illusion you become more and more detached. That very detachment gives you a tool to look at the illusion. You see it is just illusion, it does not mean anything at all – it is not intuition, it is illusion.

When I was being trained in the beginning by my Master, I would read something and think I had really understood it. I would then ask Him: "Is it a question of such and such?" And

He would say: "Exactly! Exactly." Then I would think: "I am pretty good, I got that right." Then later, with something else, I would bring my 'intuition' into play again and He would say: "Exactly." It was months before I realized that He was just saying: "Exactly." He did not mean "You are right" but, "Exactly – you said it. That is what you said". You have to learn how a Master thinks: He knows every illusion, every little trick of the mind or astral body which builds illusions and glamours. He knows them because He has seen them thousands of times before. He sees that all his disciples have them, one more than another, masses of glamours and illusions.

When we act from our heart, those actions are soul infused. How can one distinguish between acting from our emotions and acting from the heart?

That is where detachment comes in; it is a question of how detached you are – and that is a question of how experienced you are.

How to define intuition? How do we advance intuition? What is not intuition? What are the characteristics of intuition?

The characteristics of intuition are its revelatory property, its immediacy in time and space. There is no thought, no rationalization, no time. It is instant knowledge of what is. If you have it, you know. It is not as if you know and you might be right or wrong. If it is intuition, you know and you know you are right. It is a very special faculty of the soul to reveal the nature of reality.

What is it not? It is not thought-forming at all. It is not the process of thinking up great schemes. It is not the process of imagining your love for the whole of humanity. It is not in itself the process of the awareness that we are one, although that state of awareness of oneness can lead to that clarity of mind which allows the soul to demonstrate through it. It is easier to say what intuition is not than to say what it is.

Could you elaborate on how to train for intuition?

You do not sit down and train for intuition. It is the unfolding of a faculty. It makes itself felt when the mental vehicle is sufficiently clear of illusion to allow the soul to function.

No man or woman is taken on by a Master as other than a probationer who does not have the faculty of the intuition developed to some degree. They would not become an accepted disciple unless that faculty is there. It is a natural human faculty that begins to demonstrate when the soul is sufficiently infusing the bodies, and in particular the mental body, which allows the soul to throw its light on the world, the world of mentation, but also on the astral and physical plane. Then the soul can see the world as it is. But if the mind itself is full of illusion, the soul cannot see the world as it is. It gets a totally illusionary idea of the world. That is the problem for everybody.

Is being certain about anything – an idea or even knowledge gained through intuition – a sign of being illusioned?

Usually, yes. If it is intuition, you are certain. You know because you know because you know. There is no gainsaying. If you are working under illusion, you can be just as certain, but you are certain about something that is manifestly wrong. It does not relate to reality. The test is, does it relate to reality or not, or is it just an illusion, a thoughtform? When it is an illusion or thoughtform, you will find it is out of line with reality, and does not reveal anything.

Can you say something more about the courage a disciple has to have?

He has to have more courage. You need courage to tackle your glamours. It takes courage to change. Glamour, like light, has an emanation – just as wisdom or love have an emanation. It is very easy to see glamours in other people but not our own. If others have glamours, you can be sure to have glamours yourself. You are bound to have some of them. If you have, you need the courage to recognize them. It takes courage even to admit them to yourself.

Then there are the illusions of the mental plane, which any intelligent, thinking person is almost bound to have. The people in these groups are mainly, but not exclusively, intelligent, thinking people who will tend to have illusion as their main problem, rather than glamour. People suffering from illusion are usually people who have to some extent (even if they have not yet taken the second initiation) freed themselves from the glamours of the astral body, and sorted that out to a degree that they can cope with. So they need not go rushing off to the psychoanalyst!

The mind can look at the emotions and bring its light to play on the glamours of the astral body. This takes courage to do. It takes courage to change, to be ready to change, to welcome the upset, the transformation, that occurs when a person takes the first initiation, or the second or third initiations. It takes courage to get there, to get over that hump, to renounce. Mainly, evolution is a process of getting rid of things. It takes courage to change oneself and to start doing things – like Transmission Meditation. Some people are afraid of Transmission Meditation because they have heard that it changes you. They are afraid of being changed, and Transmission Meditation does change you.

In terms of dispelling glamour and illusion, would it be helpful to say the Prayer for the New Age in our daily personal meditation? If so, how does it help illuminate the mind? And would it help to visualize sweeping out the cobwebs of the mind? [For text of prayer, see back of book.]

The Prayer for the New Age is given by Maitreya to give us a sense of our reality, where we are in the scheme of things, to instil in our minds the idea of our essential divinity. If you truly have a sense of your divinity, then you do not have the glamours. It would certainly help to free the mind from these glamours. But you have to do it. You have to hold on to the response to it, what awakens in you when you say it. When you say it, it awakens a certain feeling in you. If you can hold on to that feeling for as long in the day as you can, and say it again and hold on to it, and use it in that way, it will most certainly dispel illusion in your mind. But if you just say it mechanically, I do not think you can expect much.

It would seem that so many glamours and illusions stem from the great illusion that we are separate from one another. Is 'behaving as if' or intellectually being aware of the soul, and therefore our true connection to each other, enough to transcend this illusion?

No. It is not enough to transcend the illusion, but it could be a step in the right direction. To know theoretically that we are a soul does not prevent one from being filled with glamour and illusion. To know theoretically that one is part of a human race which is one non-separate entity, not separate from any particle in the whole of cosmos, does not in itself free one from illusion.

It has to be an awareness. The only thing that frees you from illusion is awareness. That comes from experiencing yourself as a soul – you have to actually experience being a soul. When you experience yourself as a soul, you behave like a soul. You do not build up these fantasies, this phantasmagoria of illusion. Then you see clearly and do not get into the same difficulties.

When you say "someone who shows you your glamour all the time", do you mean someone else telling you what your glamour is?

No, not someone telling you what your glamour is, but relating you to the glamour at every opportunity, because unless you see it, it does not happen. As you see it, you think: "Am I really like that? Yes, I am really like that. That is precisely me." When you see this, the glamour loses its grip. Gradually with Transmission Meditation, which is service, and being active in other fields of the Reappearance work, you lose this fascination with yourself and your glamour. People love talking and thinking about themselves. Above everything else, to sit and talk about oneself, even one's glamours, is the most popular plaything in the world.

We either slough them off and say: "Well, I am going to be lost for this incarnation. I will never get beyond this glamour," or we do something about it. All we have to do really is to recognize the mechanism. Look at yourself and watch the mechanism of its action. That way you take the strength away from it, and it dissipates. Some people need somebody else to show them, but ideally you should show it to yourself.

How do our ray structures affect our tendency to glamour or illusion?

Everyone – on all rays – goes through glamour. They would not be human if they did not. Some rays are more prone to it, and some people – at the same point in evolution – are less prone to glamour, but more prone to illusion.

Rays 2-4-6 would tend probably to have more glamours – illusions that is, of an astral, emotional nature – than rays 1-3-5-7; that is not to say that rays 1-3-5-7 do not have glamours. Indeed they do.

Ray 1 has glamours and so does ray 3. Ray 5 tends to overcome glamour more quickly. It seems to be not the main problem for people of a 5th-ray mind, 5th-ray brain combination. To some extent it depends what the sub-rays are, but if the mental body is strongly influenced by the 5th ray, that person will usually suffer from illusion rather than glamour. Of course, in earlier lives the same person would suffer from illusion as glamour. People get a 5th-ray mind only when they have come to a certain point in evolution – it is little good to one earlier. The 3rd-ray person likewise has the propensity for mental stimulus – which does not mean the 3rd-ray person is free from glamour, but they will most likely build thoughtforms from the activity of the 3rd-ray on the mental body. The 1st ray has glamours when it is on the personality; you do not get many 1st-ray astrals. The 1st ray on the astral body makes for a rather cold, bossy type of person – especially if they have 6th ray elsewhere. The 1st ray on the mental body will tend to show not glamour but illusion. Sometimes these illusions are major.

Glamour in its worst expression usually lasts up to the taking of the second initiation. Most people when they are able to take the second initiation have largely overcome – using the word very loosely – the problems of glamour, but not the problems associated with illusion. Once one has taken the second initiation usually the problem of glamour is overcome, or fading away. It is not so powerful a 'disease', depending to quite a large extent on the ray structure. Certain rays, like 2, 4 and 6, for example, are very subject to glamour and, to my mind, do exhibit glamour at the second initiation or even higher. I know historically of people who were second-degree initiates who, to my mind, obviously had quite definite glamours.

The main problem of people above the second initiation is illusion. The more 'intellectual' rays – the 3rd or 5th on the mental body – are prone to illusion. The 5th-ray person can be exact, truthful and clear-thinking, because of lack of glamour, but the problem of illusion is vast for the 5th ray. The 5th-ray scientist – who believes there is nothing beyond what can be measured with instruments or seen in the microscope – sees very clearly and understands the function. He looks at the world and understands how it works; he can build models of DNA structures and can test DNA samples and trace that to an individual. All that is a function of 5th-ray type of thinking, of science. These people suffer rather from thoughtforms of knowledge; they think they know because they have analysed and studied everything. They have looked at the sky, have studied nature, the quality of the air, they know how big the solar system is, and how long it should take to get from one part of it to another, and so on. All of which may be true on one level, but it is not the truth of the nature of reality. Their illusions are huge.

That is why I call scientists – who believe that the most elaborate and beautifully constructed crop-circles worldwide are made by 'Doug and Dave', or freak winds – ignorant and arrogant. They cannot bring themselves to say: "We don't know." Those who see UFOs flying at thousands of miles an hour from one side of the sky to the other, seen by hundreds of thousands of people for years, are dismissed by the 5th-ray or 3rd-ray minded scientists, saying they know better, pretending they are flights of birds or weather balloons glowing with light, splitting into pieces, into dozens of lights, and coming together again – balloons do that!

As we become aware of, and let go of, our illusions and glamours, what relationship or effect is there on our karma?

Letting go of illusions alters our actions. Through the Law of Cause and Effect that inevitably alters our karma.

INITIATES AND ILLUSION

I believe that you said it was H.P. Blavatsky's personality and not her soul working through the Theosophical Society. How can someone who is a fourth-degree initiate, and so is a soul-infused personality, not have the soul working through their service work? Is that illusion or glamour?

It is neither illusion nor glamour. It is a simple fact that H.P. Blavatsky's soul was not involved in her work in the Theosophical Society. What was involved was her soul-infused personality. She did all of her work as a soul-infused personality. The soul of a fourth-degree initiate has been re-absorbed into the monad, so it does not exist as a separate aspect.

The personality is a vehicle for the soul, but from the monadic point of view, the soul-infused personality is not the same as the soul itself. The soul is reabsorbed by the monad at the fourth initiation, and so there is only the monad, with the soul reabsorbed, and the soul-infused personality. The energies, the powers, the qualities of the soul are expressing through the personality. The aim is for the monad to work finally through the physical-plane personality. This is achieved at the fifth initiation. The soul prepares the way, tuning up the vehicles, finer and finer, vibrating at higher and higher levels, until they can stand the union of the energies of the monad, which are so high, and the physical vehicle.

The bodies are changed subtly, gradually, by the infusion of more and more subatomic particles. By the time a person is a fourth-degree initiate, that is three-quarters subatomic and one-quarter atomic. The person is three-quarters light and one-quarter atomic matter. At the fifth initiation that process is completed, the body of the Master is 100 per cent subatomic matter or light. It is physical, but that physical is now light. We are in life to spiritualize the matter of the planet, and we do it by spiritualizing the matter aspect of our bodies. In a room of people of some initiatory standing, there is more illumination, more light in the room emanating from the bodies. If we were all Masters, it would be just one great beam of light.

A second-degree initiate should be free from glamour. Hitler was a second-degree initiate but was he free from glamour?

I do not think second-degree initiates are necessarily totally free from glamour. They are able to take the second initiation because they have achieved a relative control of the astral plane, but it does not mean that they are entirely free from glamour. However, Hitler's problem was illusion. Hitler was obsessed by two members of the Black Lodge. He was a medium and they worked through him. That is why he could pat little children on the head and his friends found him quite nice, but when he was obsessed and speaking to the people he was a raging lunatic because they were speaking through him. They took over the body and he said what they made him say. It was illusion, profound illusion. But also, if he had not been a medium it would not have happened. He probably would have had the illusions but would not have been able to carry them out. He had taken the second initiation but he was an evil personality – only an evil personality would want to rule the world and that was his aim, to rule and control the world for a thousand years. The Third Reich lasted for 12 years.

How is it possible that a bad person like Hitler could take the second initiation?

The second-degree initiate has certain power. Every initiation confers on the initiate power which you can use well or badly. It is the same power but he was a neurotic, evil personality and a medium to boot, and so could be obsessed, as he was, by members of the Black Lodge. He worked with a group of seven in Germany, together with a group of militarists in Japan and a group around Mussolini in Italy. They became the Axis Powers: the Berlin/Rome/Tokyo axis against the Allies, behind whom stood the Masters of our Hierarchy. Hitler would have dominated the world for as long as he lived – that is, not only Hitler, but the dark forces working through him. He was only an agent, an exponent of the evil, but they had to have an evil personality or evil group to send it through.

A similar thing is happening today with the Pentagon group in the United States, the Zionists in Israel and a group in eastern Europe using the same kind of energy – luckily, at a lesser potency. This war in Iraq and the general thrust of the ambitions of the US Republican government and of the Israeli government's oppression of the Palestinian people, are part of that same energetic outflow. That is why it is so dangerous. My Master has said it will take the combined strength of both Hierarchy and humanity to finally rid the world of that evil energy.

I can understand the triangle of evil in the US and Israel but what's happening in Eastern Europe?

What about Milosovic as an example? There is a group of countries in the former Eastern Bloc which is the third point of that triangle.

[Editor's note: Readers are advised to refer to the discussion particularly on glamour in *The Art of Co-operation*, Part Two 'Glamour' by Benjamin Creme.]

ILLUSION IN RELATION TO THE REAPPEARANCE GROUPS' WORK

In the attempt to reach a broader number of people with our message by de-emphasizing the more esoteric elements of that message, the concern arises that this may also diminish the potency of our outreach. There is concern that the value of such attempts may be illusionary. Can you comment?

To a certain degree I am in agreement with that statement. I have heard recently that there is a tendency, a movement almost, in this group to create an outreach that takes out of the message all the esoteric, difficult (or considered difficult) aspects. This sense of 'difficult' might be complete illusion. It is a rather patronizing view that people have of the people 'out there'. You have to consider whom you are addressing. In broad terms, it is everyone. Do you approach everyone in the same way? I would say on one level, yes, you do.

Like the television interview I did in 1982 with Merv Griffin [shown at the conference]. Everything about that was straightforward, to the point. It got through to him as a message of hope, of a highly evolved Being coming into the world with others, which was couched in some kind of esoteric, or philosophical, wording that he was not necessarily familiar with but which was not sufficiently *outré* to cause him any concern. I thought it came over very well, and so did about 15 million other people who remember it to this day and refer back to it as happening just a few years ago. It was literally about 20 years ago.

If you take out all the so-called esoteric language of the message, you are in danger of leaving out the message itself. You can diminish the message until it is no different from a nice Bible story given to children on a Sunday afternoon at the Bible class. That is not wrong, but it does not enlarge their consciousness very much. It may make them feel nice and comfortable. If that is your aim in putting forward this message, then you have certainly misunderstood mine, because that is not my aim in telling this extraordinary story.

I have no doubt that this message can be presented at different levels. There are the broad, general masses of people, millions and millions, 270 million in this country [USA]. Among these masses there will be a certain number of what you might call the educated middle classes. In this country that is a very large number indeed. In Europe, it would be probably even higher in relation to the overall population. And there are the intelligentsia. The intelligentsia in Europe, this country and Japan, for example, would be very numerous, perhaps less numerous in other countries.

There are these three broad categories: the mass of people; the middle-class educated people who make up the bulk of the Western developed nations; and the intelligentsia who are drawn from them.

I would say that the number one emphasis should be on the educated middle classes. They are ready to change. They are also, many of them, fixed in their belief systems, not looking for change, even resistant to change, but educated and generally good communicators. Many of them are open-minded, and they are the largest body of people able to understand the message in any given community.

The message should go out to them as clearly as possible, unencumbered with esoteric talk about "this will lead you to the third initiation and then you will stand before the Lord of the World". That is all right at my meetings, which have a selected audience who come for themselves, but to the general public that kind of language can be self-defeating.

But that does not mean the message itself should leave out every aspect that you might today think is esoteric. The Christ is esoteric. It is an esoteric happening. What is esoteric one day becomes exoteric another day. It is not esoteric for ever. It is not as if there is a language that belongs to the initiates. (Actually, there is a language that belongs to the initiates but we are not talking about that.)

As soon as the Christ is established in the world, and the world is living in relative peace, security and justice, He will start the restructuring and re-presentation of the mysteries. The mysteries are the mysteries of initiation which is at the very root of the New World Religion. How can you leave this out and make an intelligent approach to intelligent people as if you have something interesting and new to give? There is no use giving what other people are giving.

I have found among our literature some that is all right, nothing wrong with it, but other groups are doing more or less the same. It has the same kind of popular sounding, accommodating, non-vital message. I pick it up and read it, and put it aside. If you put it out, you want it to reveal something to others. You have to not patronize them. You have to not patronize the middle classes of today, who are at least as educated as you are. You are part of the educated middle classes of America.

You are not somehow special among them. You are doing a special work, but you are no different in consciousness, in education, and the ability to understand. You are no more open-minded, or perhaps a little more open-minded, than thousands of other groups.

You have to get it right and not patronize even the broad masses who are not educated, but whose hearts may be open and ready for the transformation which they are longing for – the fact of justice in the world, and also, potently, the fact that someone is going to bring it. The Christ is here to show people how to live. The first people to respond to Him will not be the intelligentsia or the very popular and well known journalists. They will be the millions of ordinary people in the world whose hearts will respond to His message. Give them that message and do not water it down to make it 'palatable'.

Make it tough in the sense of real. Get rid of your own illusions about who and what you are and who and what the masses of people are. Give them the benefit of the doubt. Consider that they are at least as ready as you were to hear this story and respond to it. Why not? Some will not, of course, but others will.

You cannot tell beforehand in any community who is going to respond to this message. You talk and some people come up at the end, perhaps the last person that you expected, and say: "Where can I learn more?" People are ready in a way that you do not know. That is why the Christ can be here. If it were not the case, He could not be here. Maitreya is in the world, ready and planning to emerge, to begin His open mission. He could not do it if people were not ready for it.

Maitreya hopes that we will follow His thoughts. His thoughts are not easy. The thought itself is simple: "Share the world's resources and change the world." But just to tell people, that is not enough. All people are undergoing a shift in consciousness. That is one of the results of the Christ's appearance in the world. The energies of the New Age, the Age of Aquarius, are growing in potency with every day that passes. This has a tremendous effect on the consciousness of everyone.

I think you are in danger of approaching this as you might have done 20 or 30 years ago; going back, this idea of making the teaching less esoteric, more commonplace, more easy to access. Do not get me wrong. There is a mean here, a balance, but do not go over the top, denuding it of all its meaning, because the meaning is its power.

Also, you can fill these attempts with your own illusions, especially if you are unaware of your illusions. This attempt to reach more people, but quietly, is a result, I believe, of a fear that this is a time in which you have to constrict yourself, strengthen the outer walls, consolidate rather than outreach, because there are forces that are taking away the rights of ordinary Americans to do this, that or the other. Of course, all of that is true. What is also true is that you have a right to put out this information. My advice is not to consolidate, not to restrict, to de-power and emasculate it, which is seemingly in the minds of some people.

How do you see illusion primarily manifesting in this group, and what is the overall impact on the carrying out of this group purpose? Are there specific initiatives and patterns of thought that you can highlight?

There is a kind of an alarm call. "We cannot do this. It will call attention to ourselves, so we must restrict it. We must not be too bold." My Master says the opposite. "Be bold," He says. "Be free, be strong, do not be afraid." So choose whom you want to listen to. I would rather listen to the Master.

That is a different thing from sending specific statements by the Master or me or anybody else to media whom you know are totally opposed to the whole idea, or to individuals, groups, or writers who you know have no interest in it and see it only as a tiresome interruption in their well-being. That would be stupid.

To my mind, the balance should be on the power of the message itself and not to restrict it, to give it to the general public at its middle tone, if I may put it that way. Give it to the middle classes at its most rich, and to the intellectuals at middle tone again. They are blinded by their own sense of superiority, a spurious mental superiority. That is their illusion.

Among the intellectuals in every country are some people like me. I am an intellectual. I come out of an intellectual group. All my erstwhile friends, before I got involved in this work, were painters, writers, poets, doctors, film-makers and musicians. We were the intellectuals of our specific time and place. But I think I am the only one who has become involved in this type of work. Overnight I lost most of them as friends. They disappeared into the gloaming, into their illusions. So do not expect too much from the intellectuals; you will not get far with them. Among the masses of people, in the middle classes in particular, you will find your best response.

In the work, we are confronted with the illusions of those to whom we present our information. Is it appropriate to couch the information according to the comfort level of those holding on to such illusions? Could that be hiding the truth?

That could be hiding the truth, "to couch the information according to the comfort level"! Only an American could think of that phrase! That is not used anywhere in the world but in America. The 'comfort level' of your mind. It sizes up the whole thing precisely. The comfort level must never be exceeded! Do not trespass on my comfort level! You have a little notice on your forehead with a flag that says: "Comfort level stops here." Then you get nothing above that and you feel fine. "If it is one thing I feel, that is comfortable. I did not like all that esotericism, did not feel comfortable with that. But, now I feel comfortable. This is telling me what I already know, so I feel comfortable with it."

If you reduce the message to the 'comfort level' of the majority of the people you are hoping to address, you are not going to make much headway. You are going to be popular, if that is what you want, but you are not going to get the message across.

You spoke of the duty of disciples to come forward and challenge authority and dispel illusion when possible. Likewise, the Master has encouraged us through messages to march for peace or support particular platforms. However, there is a common confusion about how much effort should be expended towards these activities at the expense of Reappearance work. This seems to be an issue for many in the group. Could you elaborate on this apparent division of effort?

To my mind there is no division. You do both. It is not that you do one at the expense of the other. You are challenging authority, dispelling illusion when possible. You are marching for peace as necessary, supporting particular platforms. But you are also using your time and energy to promote the information about the Reappearance. I do not see the division but obviously some people do.

It depends how they organize their life. If their life has to be organized and they have time measured according to so many hours for this, so many hours for that, that is one way to do it. I do not work that way, but maybe it is the way for some.

It is a question of common sense, balance. There is no other group in the world preparing the way for Maitreya and the Masters. That is the number one work. It must be given the priority.

You mentioned the need for courage on the part of the disciple to speak out the truth; should one continue to speak the truth even if it creates conflict with others?

Yes and no. If you know the truth or think you know the truth it behoves you to speak out and not pretend you do not.

On the other hand, you have to use common sense. One of the qualities most lacking in the average idealistic disciple is common sense. Then one would not get these 'hard and fast' questions needing a yes or no answer. It is not a question of yes or no; it is yes and no. Yes, if you think you know the truth, you must speak out; in so far as you know the truth it behoves you to speak the truth. But, to go around shouting your truth when nobody is listening, and when nobody wants to hear it, is another thing. You do not waste your time and energy shouting at Christian ministers: "Why don't you believe it? The Christ is in the world. How many times do I have to tell you? Why don't you as a Christian person believe this?" I know people who do this, who write to all the churches, then they write to me with the replies. It is boring and fruitless. The organized Christian and other religious groups will be the last to recognize Maitreya. The ministers do not want to hear your truth. They want to hear what is in the little book and they want to be the ones to speak. Christian ministers give a sermon every Sunday. They get no challenge from the congregation who just have to reply: "Amen," and sit down and listen. They are the last people to shout it to. Do not waste your time and energy shouting at people who do not want to hear. Common sense!

What do you see as the major illusions of the groups involved in the Reappearance work?

One of the major illusions is the notion of the exclusivity of the work. There is only a relatively small group – 3,000 to 4,000 people – who were brought into incarnation to do the Reappearance work. Because of the exceptional quality of the work (it is not every day that you prepare the way for a Christ; it is only once in 2,000 years), in the groups on the whole, if they have any illusions, one will be the illusion of grandeur, the illusion of the extraordinary value, potency and virtue of this kind of work.

I am not trying to belittle the work. The work has virtue, potency and value, I would be the last to say it did not. But if there is a tendency to illusion in respect to the work, it would be an overemphasis on the exclusiveness, the difficulty, the importance, of the work. It is only third in importance in the world. The most important groups in the world, groups with the hardest task, are the political groups. Next come the religious groups, and third come the groups preparing the world for the Reappearance. We have to get it into perspective and get a sense of proportion about it.

Another major glamour I have found is that people imagine that they are working for the Reappearance, when in reality they are not. They are interested in the Reappearance. They agree that He is here. They agree with all the facts, and they imagine that they are working for Him. Often they are not. If they are honest and look at what they do day by day, month by month, and write down how many hours per week, how many weeks per month, how many months per year they are actually working for the Reappearance, they will find it is far less than they imagine. They are interested in the Reappearance, but they are not working for the Reappearance. There is a big difference between these two statements. Most people in the groups are interested. Most people in the groups leave others to do the actual work. There are relatively few people in every group who do the work that promotes the information about the reappearance of the Christ. It is a surprising thought, but it is true.

Some people only get involved when I come to lecture. When I come, say, to America, I see the same faces every year. I say: "Oh, there is so-and-so," and I am told: "Yes, they have not been around since last time. We see them once or twice a year, just before you come. They put out some flyers." They get suddenly inspired. That gives them the right to come to the conference or to group activities.

If you are honest – and you have to be honest in this work – you will find that what I am saying is true. Many people are not involved, but think they are involved because they are interested. They mistake their interest for involvement. That is a major glamour. Involvement means doing, action, sacrifice of time and energy. That is service.

Experience shows that it is difficult to relate to others and participate in groups without sharing something of their illusion and glamour. In a way, illusion is the glue that keeps groups active. And to tackle illusion in a group means to threaten its coherence. How do you see a group working without this problem?

I can see what is meant. But why? Who said so? "In a way, illusion is the glue that keeps groups active. And to tackle illusion in a group means to threaten its coherence." I see that a group like that has a major problem. I do not agree with this at all. I think it goes on – I am not saying that it is not real. But we are talking about real groups. This is how most groups may work. That is what is meant by keeping 'comfortable' in the mind and so bringing everything down to a comfortable, acceptable level, and anything beyond that is never mentioned.

There are groups that meet and never talk about politics. They always disagree and fight, and they do not want fighting and disagreement, so they never mention politics. There are groups that meet regularly and get on very well, but they never talk about religion. They all belong to different religions and every time they talk about religion, they start fighting. So they keep 'comfortable' by accepting the glamours and illusions of these groups, but it is not groups like that I am talking about.

In this group, you can talk about politics, any kind of politics, right, left or centre, or you can talk about religion. They do not care what religion you are in. This is a different group. I am trying to point out how different an esoteric group has to be.

What characteristics might distinguish illusion at the group level beyond what the Master DK describes as affecting the individual?

At the group level you see the individual illusions magnified, because there are more people with them, and so there is a group illusion. There are also the illusions which are formed by the illusions of the strongest person, or the most bumptious, or the most talkative person in the group, who is not necessarily the strongest person, but the person who talks the most, who affects group thought most, who thinks he is the most evolved and the most responsible person to educate the group. You find that those glamours become the glamours of the group as a whole, the illusions the illusions of the group as a whole.

That can be quite subtle, happening slowly in a day-to-day way, but is nevertheless just as strong. Or it can be the strong impact of a mind which is sure of itself but filled with illusion, on minds which are filled with other illusions and make way for them. That is certainly one way in which the group illusions characterize themselves.

How do we recognize the qualities of organization versus organism? What are the signs that a group is working too much as an organization rather than an organism? Is the group moving in the right direction towards working as an organism, or is organization still a major illusion?

We recognize the qualities of an organism by its capacity to work without leadership. An organism works from itself, from the nature of the form, the life within the form manifesting its various approaches to the world, to publishing and everything connected with making known the information. If that group is functioning as an organism, it is done by individuals under the aegis of their own soul, without supervision. People are not working under somebody's supervision, like a gaffer. They work from themselves, using their own faculties and seek guidance if they need it, but otherwise do it under their own steam.

If they are truly working as an organism, what they take on, they will do. In every group there are those who will take on work and never actually complete the work. They will begin the work and leave it unfinished, and somebody else has to finish it. That is a drain on the effectiveness and energies of a group.

The major aspect of a group that works as an organism is that there is no avowed leadership. It does not depend on the power of an individual leader. It does not depend on the power of a speaker who has a louder voice and more ideas than other people. It does not depend on people who have money and therefore the ability to put their resources, their house, their cars, for the benefit of the group. There are those who claim benefits, who claim residence in the group from right of money. They provide a meeting place, they provide facilities because they have the ability to do that. That is accepted, but it does not provide any rights. If the group is working as an organism, it will not.

If the group is working as an organization, then it might and very often does. An organization will be distinguished by the fact of there being people in charge. There will be people who control the ideas, the outflow of ideas, the ways in which ideas are written. That will be an organization rather like the organization in the outer field in business. The group will equate more and more to business, as the people involved in it come out of a business milieu and know these routines and adapt the routines to this kind of group.

This group is an entirely new kind of group and does not work well when it is organized in that way. A certain degree of organization is necessary in any group which is bigger than two or three people. But that degree of organization should be kept to a minimum and should simply be the outcome of the demand coming from outside. When the demand is high, you expand the organizational capacity to meet the demand. When the demand is not high, you do not.

An organization will work another way and create an organization which is built to supply a large amount of information whether there is a demand for it or not. When it gets bigger, it is able to supply it. When it is slow, they are stuck with this organization which is, to a degree, not in use. There are other differences I am sure. Some of them will occur to you which do not occur to me. But the aim of all organizations is to get bigger, more and more powerful, more and more known, as a powerful voice in the world.

Our purpose is making known the appearance of Maitreya and the Masters in the world to the best of our ability, which means on the widest possible scale. That, to my mind, is best done like my television interview with Merv Griffin. That reached, apparently, 15 million people. There is nothing special about the interview. It is neither better nor worse than hundreds of others that took place before and since. But it was on the Merv Griffin show, and he had a 15-million-strong audience. Numbers tell. The best way for any group to work is to reach audiences through television. In one 20-minute or half-hour interview, you can reach millions of people. If you speak simply and properly, you can be very potent and effective. It is the most potent instrument of communication that we have, which is why all the world leaders use it on every occasion.

[Editor's note: For the discussion on organism vs. organization in terms of how the group should function, see *The Art of Co-operation,* Part Two 'Glamour' by Benjamin Creme.]

SPIRITUAL TENSION

What is the importance of spiritual tension in ridding ourselves of glamour and illusion?

Without spiritual tension we would not have the spiritual insight. The spiritual insight which we have we probably think comes from books or from hearing people speak. This we call our spiritual ideas and ideals. We live our life in relation to these, but pay not too much heed to the idea of spiritual tension. How do we know that these spiritual ideas and ideals are not themselves simply illusion? We can only recognize illusion from the spiritual insight which comes as a result of building up a spiritual tension.

Spiritual tension is not continuous in most people throughout their lives. It is not something we are given and once we have it, we have it. It is like a clock which constantly needs winding up. As time goes on it unwinds until it can hardly turn the hands and we have to wind it up again. The spiritual batteries have likewise to be wound up and this is the value of meditation, above all, of Transmission Meditation.

Spiritual tension is the outcome of spiritual aspiration and service – meditation, or work connected with the emergence of Maitreya and the Masters, work which has a spiritual ideal as the generating energy for the work. The spiritual tension reaches a point which can then be seen in some creativity, when creativity is the result, when you have built up the spiritual tension to a point when the pressure forces you into spiritual action. And it is action. It is not going around with a lovely sense of yourself as a 'spiritual person'. It is nothing to do with that; that is mainly glamour. This sense that one is a spiritual person, always looking slightly upwards, rolling the eyes and always talking quietly, never laughing out loud, only in a genteel manner, never saying anything strong or rude, or conflicting with other people, being 'spiritual' – that is glamour. Even the idea of 'being spiritual' is a glamour. If you are spiritual you do not think about it.

The spiritual batteries are charged by spiritual thoughts and spiritual thoughts are creativity. It is not thinking nice thoughts; it is being creative in whatever manner one is creative. That builds up spiritual tension. Meditation builds up spiritual tension, especially Transmission Meditation. It is action of a spiritual nature, and I do not mean that as what is normally called 'good' action – of course it will be good if it is spiritual action. But it does not have to be self-consciously good or 'spiritual'. It is action for the good of the world. Whatever transforms the world into a better state; every such action is spiritual whether it is on the physical, emotional, mental, or soul plane. Whatever brings the person or humanity as a whole to a higher level is fundamentally spiritual.

TRANSMISSION MEDITATION

A BRIEF EXPLANATION

A group meditation providing both a dynamic service to the world and powerful, personal spiritual development.

Transmission Meditation is a group meditation established better to distribute spiritual energies from their Custodians, the Masters of Wisdom, our planetary Spiritual Hierarchy. It is a means of 'stepping down' (transforming) these energies so that they become accessible and useful to the general public. It is the creation, in co-operation with the Hierarchy of Masters, of a vortex or pool of higher energy for the benefit of humanity.

In March 1974, under the direction of his Master, Benjamin Creme formed the first Transmission Meditation group in London. Today there are hundreds of Transmission Meditation groups around the world and new groups are forming all the time.

Transmission Meditation groups provide a link whereby Hierarchy can respond to world need. The prime motive of this work is service, but it also constitutes a powerful mode of personal growth. Many people are searching for ways in which to improve the world; this desire to serve can be strong, but difficult, in our busy lives, to fulfil. Our soul needs a means to serve, but we do not always respond to its call, and so produce disequilibrium and conflict within ourselves. Transmission Meditation provides a unique opportunity for service in a potent and fully scientific way with the minimum expenditure of one's time and energy.

Benjamin Creme holds Transmission Meditation workshops around the world. During the meditation he is overshadowed by Maitreya, the World Teacher, which allows Maitreya to confer great spiritual nourishment on the participants. Many people are inspired to begin Transmission Meditation after attending such a workshop, and many acknowledge having received healing in the process.

[Please refer to Benjamin Creme, *Transmission: A Meditation for the New Age,* Share International Foundation]

THE PRAYER FOR THE NEW AGE

I am the creator of the universe.
I am the father and mother of the universe.
Everything came from me.
Everything shall return to me.
Mind, spirit and body are my temples,
For the Self to realize in them
My supreme Being and Becoming.

The Prayer for the New Age, given by Maitreya, the World Teacher, is a great mantram or affirmation with an invocative effect. It will be a powerful tool in the recognition by us that man and God are One, that there is no separation. The 'I' is the Divine Principle behind all creation. The Self emanates from, and is identical to, the Divine Principle.

The most effective way to use this mantram is to say or think the words with focused will, while holding the attention at the ajna centre between the eyebrows. When the mind grasps the meaning of the concepts, and simultaneously the will is brought to bear, those concepts will be activated and the mantram will work. If it is said seriously every day, there will grow inside you a realization of your true Self.

THE GREAT INVOCATION

From the point of Light within the Mind of God
Let light stream forth into the minds of men.
Let Light descend on Earth.

From the point of Love within the Heart of God
Let love stream forth into the hearts of men.
May Christ return to Earth.

From the centre where the Will of God is known
Let purpose guide the little wills of men –
The purpose which the Masters know and serve.

From the centre which we call the race of men
Let the Plan of Love and Light work out
And may it seal the door where evil dwells.

Let Light and Love and Power restore
the Plan on Earth.

The Great Invocation, used by the Christ for the first time in June 1945, was released by Him to humanity to enable man himself to invoke the energies which would change our world, and make possible the return of the Christ and Hierarchy. This is not the form of it used by the Christ. He uses an ancient formula, seven mystic phrases long, in an ancient sacerdotal tongue. It has been translated (by Hierarchy) into terms which we can use and understand, and, translated into many languages, is used today in every country in the world.

It can be made even more potent in the form of triangles, as in the Triangles Movement (of the Lucis Trust). If you wish to work in this way, arrange with two friends to use the Invocation, aloud, daily. You need not be in the same town, or country, or say it at the same time of day. Simply say it when convenient for each one, and, linking up mentally with the two other members, visualize a triangle of white light circulating above your heads and see it linked to a network of such triangles, covering the world.

Another way, which can be used in conjunction with the triangle, is the following:

When you say the first line: "From the point of Light . . . ," visualize (or think of, if you cannot visualize Him) the Buddha, the Embodiment of Light or Wisdom on the Planet. Visualize Him sitting in the Lotus posture, saffron robe over one shoulder, hand raised in blessing, and see emanating from the heart centre, the ajna centre (between the eyebrows), and the upraised hand of the Buddha, a brilliant golden light. See this light enter the minds of men everywhere.

When you say the line: "Let Light descend on Earth," visualize the Sun, the physical Sun, and see emanating from it beams of white light. See this light enter and saturate the Earth.

When you say: "From the point of Love . . . ," visualize the Christ (the Embodiment of Love) however you see Him. A good way is to see Him standing at the head of an inverted Y-shaped table, thus: 人, each arm of the 人 of the same length. (That table exists in the world, and the Christ presides at it.) See Him standing, arms raised in blessing, and see emanating from the heart centre and the upraised hands of the Christ, a brilliant rose-coloured light (not red). Visualize this rose light enter the hearts of men everywhere.

When you say the line: "May Christ return to Earth," remember that this refers to the Hierarchy as a whole and not only to the Christ. He is the heart centre of the Hierarchy, and although He is now among us, the remainder of the Hierarchy (that part of it which will externalize slowly, over the years) still requires to be invoked, the magnetic conduit for Their descent has still to be maintained.

When you say: "From the centre where the Will of God is known . . .," which is Shamballa, visualize a great sphere of white light. (You can place it, mentally, in the Gobi desert, where it is, on the two highest of the four etheric planes. One day, when mankind develops etheric vision which it will do in this coming age, this centre will be seen and known, as many other etheric centres will be seen and known.) Streaming from this sphere of brilliant light visualize, again, beams of light entering the world, galvanizing mankind into spiritual action.

Do this with focused thought and intention, your attention fixed on the ajna centre between the eyebrows. In this way you form a telepathic conduit between yourselves and Hierarchy. Through that conduit the energies thus invoked can flow. The Great Invocation is used in this way at the start of every Transmission Meditation. There is nothing better you can do for the world or yourselves, than channel these great spiritual potencies.

BOOKS BY BENJAMIN CREME

The Reappearance of the Christ and the Masters of Wisdom

In his first book, Benjamin Creme gives the background and pertinent information concerning the emergence of Maitreya (the Christ), as World Teacher for the New Age now dawning. Expected under different names by all religious groups, Maitreya comes to help us create co-operation among the many ideological factions, galvanize world goodwill and sharing, and inspire sweeping political, social, economic and environmental reforms. Benjamin Creme puts the most profound event of the last 2,000 years into its correct historical and esoteric context and describes what effect the World Teacher's presence will have on both the world's institutions and the average person. Through his telepathic contact with a Master of Wisdom, Creme offers insights on such subjects as the soul and reincarnation; fear of death; telepathy; meditation; nuclear energy; ancient civilizations; UFOs; problems of the developing world; a new economic order; the Antichrist; and the 'Last Judgement'.

1st edition 1979. ISBN 0-936604-00-X, 254pp.

Messages from Maitreya the Christ

During the years of preparation for His emergence, Maitreya gave 140 Messages through Benjamin Creme during public lectures in London from 1977 to 1982. The method used was mental overshadowing and a telepathic rapport thus set up.

Maitreya's Messages of sharing, co-operation and unity inspire readers to spread the news of His reappearance and to work urgently for the rescue of millions suffering from poverty and starvation in a world of plenty. In Message No. 11

Maitreya says: "*My Plan is to show you that the way out of your problems is to listen again to the true voice of God within your hearts, to share the produce of this most bountiful of worlds among your brothers and sisters everywhere. . . .*" Maitreya's words are a unique source of wisdom, hope and succour at this critical time of world change, and when read aloud these profound yet simple Messages invoke His energy and blessing.

1st edition Vol. I 1981, Vol. II 1986. 2nd, combined, edition 1992, reprinted 2001. ISBN 90-71484-22-X, 286pp.

Transmission: A Meditation for the New Age

Transmission Meditation is a form of group meditation for the purpose of 'stepping down' (transforming) spiritual energies which thus become accessible and useful to the general public. It is the creation, in co-operation with the Hierarchy of Masters, of a vortex or pool of higher energy for the benefit of humanity.

Introduced in 1974 by Benjamin Creme, under the direction of his Master, this is a form of service which is simple to do and is at the same time a powerful means of personal growth. The meditation is a combination of two yogas: Karma Yoga (yoga of service) and Laya Yoga (yoga of energy or chakras). It is a service in which we can be involved for the rest of our lives knowing that we are helping the evolution of humanity into, and beyond, the New Age. There are hundreds of Transmission Meditation groups active in many countries around the world.

In this practical and inspiring book Benjamin Creme describes the aims, technique and results of Transmission Meditation, as well as the underlying purpose of the meditation for the development of disciples.

1st edit. 1983. 5th edit. 2006. ISBN 90-71484-35-1,212 pp.

A Master Speaks

Humanity is guided from behind the scenes by a highly evolved and illumined group of men Who have preceded us along the path of evolution. These Masters of Wisdom, as They are called, seldom appear openly, but usually work through Their disciples – men and women who influence society through their work in science, education, art, religion, politics, and in every department of life.

British artist Benjamin Creme is a disciple of a Master with Whom he is in close telepathic contact. Since the launching of *Share International*, the magazine of which Benjamin Creme is editor, his Master has contributed to every issue an inspiring article on a wide range of subjects: reason and intuition; the new civilization; health and healing; the art of living; the need for synthesis; justice is divine; the Son of Man; human rights; the law of rebirth; the end of hunger; sharing for peace; the rise of people power; the brightest future; co-operation – and many more.

The major purpose of these articles is to draw attention to the needs of the present and the immediate future time, and to give information about the teachings of Maitreya, the Master of all the Masters. This third edition contains all 223 articles from the first 22 volumes of *Share International*.
1st edition 1985. 3rd expanded edition 2004. ISBN 90-71484-29-7, 452pp.

Maitreya's Mission, Volume One

The first of a trilogy of books which describe the emergence and teachings of Maitreya, the World Teacher. As human consciousness steadily matures, many of the ancient 'mysteries' are now being revealed. This volume can be seen as a guidebook for humanity as it travels on the evolutionary journey. The book's canvas is vast: from the new teachings of the Christ to meditation and karma; from life after death, and reincarnation, to healing and social transformation; from initiation and the role of service to the Seven Rays; from Leonardo da Vinci and Mozart to Sathya Sai Baba. It sets the scene and prepares the way for the work of Maitreya, as World Teacher, and the creation of a new and better life for all. It is a powerful message of hope.

1st edition 1986. 3rd edition 1993, reprinted 2003. ISBN 90-71484-08-4, 419pp.

Maitreya's Mission, Volume Two

This inspiring and heart-warming book offers new hope and guidance to a suffering world on the threshold of a Golden Age. It presents the teachings of Maitreya, the World Teacher, on both the outer, practical, and inner, spiritual levels; His uniquely accurate forecasts of world events, which have astonished international media; and His miraculous appearances which have brought hope and inspiration to many thousands. It also contains a series of unique interviews with Benjamin Creme's Master which throw new and revealing light on some of the greatest problems facing humanity.

This book covers an enormous range: Maitreya's teachings; the growth of consciousness; new forms of government; commercialization and market forces; the principal of sharing; life in the New Age; schools without walls; the Technology of Light; crop circles; the Self; telepathy; disease and death; energy and thought; Transmission Meditation; the soul's purpose. Also includes transcripts of Benjamin Creme's inspiring talks on 'The Overcoming of Fear' and 'The Call to Service'.

1st edition 1993, reprinted 2004. ISBN 90-71484-11-4, 753pp.

Maitreya's Mission, Volume Three

Benjamin Creme presents a compelling vision of the future. With Maitreya, the World Teacher, and His disciples the Masters of Wisdom openly offering Their guidance, humanity will create a civilization worthy of its divine potential. Peace will be established; sharing the world's resources the norm; maintaining our environment a top priority. The new education will teach the fact of the soul and the evolution of consciousness. The cities of the world will be transformed into centres of great beauty.

This book offers invaluable wisdom on a vast range of topics. It includes Maitreya's priorities for the future, and interviews with a Master of Wisdom on 'The Challenge of the 21st Century'. It explores karma and reincarnation, the origin of humanity, meditation and service, the Plan of evolution, and other fundamental concepts of the Ageless Wisdom Teachings. It includes a fascinating look from an esoteric, spiritual perspective at 10 famous artists – among them Leonardo da Vinci, Michelangelo and Rembrandt – by Benjamin Creme, himself an artist.

Like the first two volumes of *Maitreya's Mission*, this work combines profound spiritual truths with practical solutions to today's most vexing problems. It is indeed a message of hope for a humanity ready to "begin the creation of a civilization such as this world has never yet seen".

1st edition 1997. ISBN 90-71484-15-7, 705pp.

The Great Approach: New Light and Life for Humanity

This prophetic book addresses the problems of our chaotic world and its gradual change under the influence of a group of perfected men, the Masters of Wisdom, Who, with Their leader Maitreya, the World Teacher, are returning openly to the world for the first time in 98,000 years.

The book covers such topics as: sharing; the USA in a quandary; ethnic conflicts; crime and violence; environment and pollution; genetic engineering; science and religion; the nature of light; health and healing; education; miracles; the soul and incarnation. An extraordinary synthesis of knowledge, it throws a searchlight on the future; with clear vision it predicts our highest achievements of thought to reveal the amazing scientific discoveries which lie ahead. It shows us a world in which war is a thing of the past, and the needs of all are met.

1st edition 2001. ISBN 90-71484-23-8, 320pp.

The Art of Co-operation

The Art of Co-operation deals with the most pressing problems of our time, and their solution, from the point of view of the Ageless Wisdom Teachings that, for millennia, have revealed the forces underlying the outer world. Benjamin Creme brings these teachings up to date, preparing the way for the imminent emergence of Maitreya, the World Teacher, and His group of Masters of Wisdom.

This volume looks at a world locked in ancient competition, trying to solve its problems by old and out-worn methods, while the answer – co-operation – lies in our own hands. It shows the way to a world of justice, freedom and peace through a growing appreciation of the unity underlying all life. Maitreya will inspire in us this growing realization.

Topics include: the necessity of co-operation; the USA and competition; organism versus organization; opportunity for service; fear of loss; karma; love; courage and detachment; overcoming of glamour; how the Masters teach; unity in diversity; consensus; trust.

1st edition 2002. ISBN 90-71484-26-2, 235pp.

Maitreya's Teachings: The Laws of Life

We do not have even fragments of the teachings of former World Teachers given prior to certain knowledge of Their existence. We do not have the teachings of a Christ, or a Buddha, or a Krishna, except seen through the eyes of later followers. For the first time we are given the flavour of the thoughts and insights of a Being of immeasurable stature to enable us to understand the path of evolution stretching ahead of us which He has come to outline for us. The impression left in the mind by the Teacher is that the breadth and depth of His knowledge and awareness have no limits; that He is tolerant and wise beyond conception, and of amazing humility.

Few could read from these pages without being changed. To some the extraordinary insights into world events will be of major interest, while to others the laying bare of the secrets of self-realization, the simple description of experienced truth, will be a revelation. To anyone seeking to understand the Laws of Life, these subtle and pregnant insights will take them quickly to the core of Life itself, and provide them with a simple path stretching to the mountain-top. The essential unity of all life is underscored in a clear and meaningful way. Never, it would appear, have the Laws by which we live seemed so natural and so unconstraining.

1st edition, 2005. ISBN 90-71484-31-9, 258pp.

The Ageless Wisdom Teaching

An overview of humanity's spiritual legacy, this booklet serves as a concise and easy-to-understand introduction to the Ageless Wisdom Teaching. It explains the basic tenets of esotericism, including: source of the Teaching; the emergence of the World Teacher; rebirth and reincarnation; the Law of Cause and Effect; the Plan of evolution; origin of man; meditation and service; future changes. Also included is an esoteric glossary and a recommended reading list.

1st edition 1996, reprinted 2006. ISBN 90-71484-13-0, 76pp.

The above books are published by Share International Foundation (Amsterdam, London, Los Angeles). Most have been translated and published in Dutch, French, German, Japanese and Spanish by groups responding to this message. Some have also been published in Chinese, Croatian, Finnish, Greek, Hebrew, Italian, Portuguese, Romanian, Russian, Slovenian and Swedish. Further translations are planned. Books, as well as audio and video cassettes, are available from local booksellers.

SHARE INTERNATIONAL

A unique magazine featuring each month: up-to-date information about the emergence of Maitreya, the World Teacher; an article from a Master of Wisdom; expansions of the esoteric teachings; Benjamin Creme's answers to a wide variety of topical and esoteric questions; articles by and interviews with people at the forefront of progressive world change; news from UN agencies and reports of positive developments in the transformation of our world.

Share International brings together the two major directions of New Age thinking – the political and the spiritual. It shows the synthesis underlying the political, social, economic and spiritual changes now occurring on a global scale, and seeks to stimulate practical action to rebuild our world along more just and compassionate lines.

Share International covers news, events and comments related to Maitreya's priorities: an adequate supply of the right food, housing and shelter for all, healthcare and education as universal rights, and the maintenance of ecological balance in the world. *ISSN 0169-1341*

Versions of *Share International* are available in Dutch, French, German, Japanese, Romanian, Slovenian and Spanish. For subscription information, contact the appropriate office below.

For North, Central and South America, Australia,
New Zealand and the Philippines
Share International
PO Box 971, North Hollywood, CA 91603, USA

For the UK
Share International
PO Box 3677, London NW5 1RU, UK

For the rest of the world
Share International
PO Box 41877, 1009 DB Amsterdam, Holland

Extensive information and excerpts from the magazine are published online at: www.share-international.org

INDEX

ABOUT THE AUTHOR

Scottish-born painter and esotericist Benjamin Creme has for over 30 years been preparing the world for the most extraordinary event in human history – the return of our spiritual mentors to the everyday world.

Benjamin Creme has appeared on television, radio and in documentary films worldwide, and lectures throughout Western and Eastern Europe, the USA, Japan, Australia, New Zealand, Canada and Mexico.

Trained and supervised over many years by his own Master, he began his public work in 1974. In 1982 he announced that the Lord Maitreya, the long-awaited World Teacher, was living in London, ready to present Himself openly when invited by the media to do so. This event is now imminent.

Benjamin Creme continues to carry out his task as messenger of this inspiring news. His books, eleven at present, have been translated into many languages. He is also the editor of *Share International* magazine, which circulates in over 70 countries. He accepts no money for any of this work.

Benjamin Creme lives in London, is married, and has three children.